"An investment in knowledge pays the best interest."

– Benjamin Franklin

BLOCKCHAIN INVESTING

BY

FRANK D. FUTURIST

ABOUT THE AUTHOR

FRANK D. FUTURIST

BRITISH ACADEMIC &
BASED IN LONDON,
ENGLAND.

WE’RE IN THE CHANGING LIVES BUSINESS.

WANT FREE GOODIES?

EMAIL ME AT:
mindsetmastership@gmail.com

FIND US ON INSTAGRAM!

@MINDSETMASTERSHIP

MASTERSHIP BOOKS
UK | USA | CANADA | IRELAND | AUSTRALIA
INDIA | NEW ZEALAND | SOUTH AFRICA | CHINA
MASTERSHIP BOOKS IS PART OF THE UNITED ARTS PUBLISHING HOUSE
GROUP OF COMPANIES BASED IN LONDON, ENGLAND, UK.

FIRST PUBLISHED BY MASTERSHIP BOOKS (LONDON, UK), 2021
I S B N: 9 7 8 1 9 1 5 0 0 2 0 2 0

COVER DESIGN BY RICH © UNITED ARTS PUBLISHING (UK)
TEXT AND INTERNAL DESIGN BY RICH © UNITED ARTS PUBLISHING (UK)
IMAGE CREDITS RESERVED.
COLOUR SEPARATION BY SPITTING IMAGE DESIGN STUDIO
PRINTED AND BOUND IN GREAT BRITAIN
NATIONAL PUBLICATIONS ASSOCIATION OF BRITAIN
LONDON, ENGLAND, UNITED KINGDOM.
PAPER DESIGN UAP
ISBN: 978-1-915002-02-0

(PAPERBACK)
A723.5
TITLE: **BLOCKCHAIN INVESTING**
DESIGN, BOUND & PRINTED:
LONDON, ENGLAND, GREAT BRITAIN.

CONTENTS

0

INTRODUCTION

Blockchain Introduction

Before diving into the details of the book, this Introduction aims to provide an overview of some of the major concepts by describing how blockchain works.

A recent report by Deloitte identified five key concepts for blockchain:

1. Blocks: Each block contains data including the hash of the previous block, a timestamp, and transaction data created by users.
2. Transactions. Typically, transactions contain details about the sender and receiver of a Bitcoin payment as well as additional details such as an amount or purpose of payment
3. Creation. Users create the blocks, which make up a blockchain. Anyone can be a block creator by installing software although the process is resource-intensive and only highly technical users typically create blocks.

4. Verification: The block creators have to demonstrate that they have done some work before their blocks can be added to the chain of previous blocks. This is to ensure that there isn't fraud such as the same transaction being added more than once. It is also to ensure that no one with malicious intent can take control of the flow of Bitcoins and change individual transactions or forge new blocks.

5. Security: The block creators have to prove their own identity by solving a mathematical problem using cryptographic hashing functions in order to be able to create blocks (they receive a reward for their work). The very fact that the block creators are different people and they don't know each other means that it is more difficult to conduct fraudulent transactions.

When writing about technology such as blockchain, it is important to make it clear from the beginning that there are many different viewpoints about what is going on with digital currency and which new technologies are emerging.

In order to understand blockchain, I would also add another concept: the consensus process by which decisions about updating the chain of blocks are made. Decisions on updating the chain of blocks are made by a majority vote. The system is designed to ensure that decisions about adding new blocks to the chain happen as frequently as possible.

One of the big issues for blockchain is how anonymous all of this is meant to be, or rather isn't meant to be. Users identify themselves by cryptographic keys and transactions are made anonymously. This is in contrast to say a bank account where the ownership of an account can be known because it was opened with a social security or national insurance number. It is this anonymity that has led to blockchain being viewed as favorable by people who like privacy, for example, criminals, but also from countries such as China and Russia where citizens' details are not well protected by governments.

The value of Bitcoin and other cryptocurrencies depends on public confidence. When large sums move in or out of Bitcoin exchanges within minutes then confidence can quickly disappear. The more that banks and other financial institutions show interest in blockchain technology, the stronger the belief becomes that digital currency will become strong enough to be used by mainstream businesses and consumers.

If cryptocurrencies such as Bitcoin become widely used for purchasing goods, then there needs to be much more energy invested into the mining process which creates blocks. Currently, the consensus process doesn't work properly because not enough new blocks are created, meaning users find confirmation times slow down considerably. There have been suggestions for ways around this but these might prove controversial amongst some users of cryptocurrency. To understand why this is necessary we need to turn back to look at how blockchain works.

Users who use cryptographic keys make transactions. These users must also solve mathematical problems using other cryptographic keys in order to be able to create a block. When a new block is created, the user that created it receives Bitcoins as a reward. Because there are more transactions than blocks being created, the waiting time for coins to be transferred from one person to another gets longer and longer. In addition, because of an arms race between Bitcoin miners (people creating new blocks) and Bitcoin Cash miners (those trying to make their blockchain smaller), the computing power needed so that new blocks can be created has increased considerably with mining now requiring purpose-built computers rather than standard PCs. As these computers require more energy they spend more money on electricity, which puts them at a disadvantage compared to larger mining companies with access to lower-cost electricity.

Working out how energy requirements can be lowered will require another arms race between miners. One idea is that smaller amounts of Bitcoins could be rewarded for creating new blocks, which would reduce the power needed by miners and lead to less money being spent on electricity. A lot of controversy has been caused by this idea because it goes against Bitcoin's original design principle of rewarding people who are first to create new blocks with the most Bitcoins as prizes. Other ideas include eliminating transaction fees but if there are no fees then there seems little point in having cryptocurrency such as Bitcoin in the first place as fiat currency (money issued by central banks) already works perfectly well without needing transaction fees.

The idea of rewarding people who are first to create new blocks with the most Bitcoins as prizes have another effect. In the beginning, when Bitcoin was launched, users ran mining software on their computers and received Bitcoins as rewards for being the first to create new blocks. Today, high-powered mining computers have been built especially just so that they can mine Bitcoin faster than using a standard PC or laptop. This has led to an arms race between miners which means computer manufacturers (who sell these specially designed machines) invest a lot of money into developing machines that will give them an advantage over competitors' products and miners spend lots of money on building bigger farms (or collections) of computers to allow them to generate more reward coins quicker than their competitors (by being able to create new blocks sooner). If the reward for creating new blocks is reduced then all of this effort will have been for nothing because miners will need to find other ways of recouping their costs.

It's not just Bitcoin that has this problem of expensive computers and large amounts of electricity being used. Any cryptocurrency that uses proof-of-work consensus needs more energy than the amount consumed by a standard computer would in order to work properly. As such, cryptocurrencies offer a solution to our problems with creating trust on the Internet but at considerable cost as well. For example, there are an estimated 2,000 Bitcoin mining servers located within The Dells region alone (an area close to where I live) which means that the electricity used by these computers alone must be colossal. This is in addition to the normal energy consumption of all the other data centers that are also located close by. That's a lot of power and money being used for what was meant to be a cheaper alternative to fiat currency (which can be created at no cost whatsoever).

The problem with using proof-of-work consensus for creating trust on the Internet is that it uses so much more energy than a standard computer would use as part of its process. The question then becomes how much energy do we need to use if we want to create trust between strangers on the Internet?

Blockchain and bitcoin are just two use-cases for consensus mechanisms based on proof-of-work.

The cryptocurrencies all use the blockchain technology developed by Bitcoin but they often have very different ideas about how much power should be used (in order to create trust over the internet). For example, DigiByte uses five billion times more power than Bitcoin in order to achieve consensus and the newer cryptocurrencies like Cardano (which promises to use even less electricity than DigiByte) are still needlessly wasteful compared to a traditional database system, which can create trust as well. As it stands, there seems no reason for why we would ever want to replace our traditional databases with blockchain technology apart from being able to tell people that you're using a really cool piece of technology!

However, the use cases for blockchain are not limited to cryptocurrencies. The blockchain also offers a way of creating decentralized systems, which can be used for many different kinds of applications such as the creation of decentralized apps (dApps) and platforms. These are built on top of the Ethereum platform and they use a slightly different kind of consensus mechanism called proof-of-stake. Contrary to proof-of-work's requirement that machines show their work in order to prove that blocks must have been created by competent miners, proof-of-stake simply requires coins held by validators...

The same amount of energy is being used here but it costs much less money if we price it per transaction instead.

The idea of using blockchain technology for creating trust has been around for a long time before Bitcoin was launched. In fact, there are many alternative cryptocurrencies (such as Namecoin, Peercoin, Litecoin etc.) which all use some other type of consensus mechanism instead of proof-of-work. For example, most miners can also earn money from mining bitcoin but they can also set up their computers to mine other cryptocurrencies based on SHA256 such as Namecoin or others that are based on Scrypt like Dogecoins in order to earn profit.

As we saw earlier, energy consumption is an issue; however as electricity costs start to decline over time with new infrastructure the blockchain space could change rapidly.

In sum, this introduction to blockchain technology has shown that proof-of-work is a very inefficient method of providing trust on the Internet. If we want to use blockchain technology as part of our mission to build decentralized systems and create a more open Internet, then we should be aiming for less energy usage by using newer consensus algorithms such as proof-of-stake or even better would be if we could find a way of creating trust without needing to waste any computational power at all (as this would be the only way in which the blockchain can really help us meet our goals).

1

WHAT IS MONEY?

What is Money?

Money is a complex topic with no single definition but it all comes down to one simple principle: you can use money to buy things that were made by other people.

Physical and Digital Money

Physical money can be anything from gold to paper, a coin or a banknote. It is often referred to as commodity money and it is most valuable when its price doesn't change much over time. The next most valuable type of physical currency that we have today are banknotes (such as dollar bills) which are fiat currencies and there values are determined by the central banks who issue them... Until they lose trust in times of economic crises! So, it turns out that these pieces of paper only maintain value because people believe in them: this is something we call confidence. On the other hand, if all people stop believing in the currency, then it would quickly become useless which has happened with many different forms of physical money throughout history.

Bitcoin is a form of digital currency that is backed by no physical commodity. It has been designed to be completely decentralized and not regulated by any government or other central authority so it's price cannot be easily manipulated.

Another key aspect of bitcoin as money is that you can send it anywhere in the world instantly, without needing an intermediary like a bank to manage transactions. This means that people are now able to store their money themselves instead of trusting a centralized third party with their savings which have proved vulnerable time and time again throughout history (most notably during the latest recession when huge numbers of people lost trust in banks).

Despite all this, there doesn't seem to be much demand for bitcoins... In fact, most people don't even know how to use it! There are currently just over 18.6 Billion bitcoins in circulation around the world (as of March 2021), and this number will never change which means that there is a maximum of 21 million bitcoins that can ever exist. Whilst we've only seen 4 million or so bitcoin transactions per day, this number has been steadily increasing for the past couple of years.

This idea for using a decentralized currency with no tangible value, as money might sound strange but it actually makes complete sense from an economic point of view... Bitcoin is simply better money than any other form because it enables the creation of trust between strangers on the Internet whilst relying on a much cheaper mechanism (mining) instead of a more expensive one (a central bank). However, if you still don't see the economic argument behind bitcoins then look at it this way: If you need to buy a $10,000 house online in the USA, how would you do that today? Would you trust an intermediary (such as a bank or government) to handle your money for you and facilitate that transaction? Or would you rather use Bitcoin so that both the seller and buyer have equal control over their funds at all times?

Key differences to know with physical and digital money.

Physical money is based on trust between strangers. Digital money can be decentralized so you don't have to rely on strangers. Physical money is centralized and so it can be easily manipulated by governments to control the economy or the flow of information. Digital money cannot be centralized because every single person has equal power over his or her funds at all times. Physical money requires a central authority for issuing new units, controlling transactions and guaranteeing that each unit has enough value (backed by the government). Digital currency does not require a central issuing authority. In fact, digital currency doesn't need any kind of issuing authority whatsoever because people can create trust amongst themselves using mathematics and code instead!

Bitcoin also creates an extremely resilient system without requiring much trust because it relies on cryptography. By taking advantage of the fact that every single person has access to a global platform for money, it's possible to create a system where two people anywhere on Earth can trust each other without needing to rely on any kind of intermediary. This is why bitcoin can enable true peer-to-peer commerce online and makes all kinds of interactions between strangers cheaper and more convenient than ever before.

The implications behind this are massive... It means that we could potentially see many new marketplaces emerge in areas where there isn't currently competition (such as digital goods) because sellers will no longer have to pay expensive fees to banks or centralized services that used to be responsible for holding their funds and facilitating transactions. There are also many different kinds of industries and services in today's world that rely on middlemen so if we get rid of these problems then there is a good chance that we will see online commerce become much more streamlined and efficient as a result.

If you don't believe this theory or think that bitcoin is just an overhyped fad, it's worth pointing out that the first era of the Internet (from the late 90's to early 2000's) was full of people who used to say similar things... It's now as it turns out were some pretty huge changes have taken place!

Bitcoin is still in its infancy (despite being only several years old) but I truly believe that it has the potential to be 'the next big thing' in the online world. There is a lot of hype and misinformation surrounding this technology at the moment but I don't think that will be the case forever...

2

THE BLOCKCHAIN TECHNOLOGY

The Blockchain Technology

The concept of blockchain was invented by Satoshi Nakamoto back in 2008. This is the same person who wrote the whitepaper on Bitcoin outlining his real-time peer-to-peer electronic cash system. As we discussed earlier, he used proof-of-work to create a monetary incentive for miners to verify transactions on the network.

However, there is actually a lot more to blockchain technology than just bitcoin! The blockchain itself is an open, distributed ledger that can record transactions between two parties efficiently and in a verifiable manner. Ledger data can be easily proven incorrect through logic and mathematics so it's incredibly difficult for anyone to change or falsify records without getting caught. When used as designed, blockchains are thus far less prone to errors and fraud than ordinary databases which makes them ideal not only for recording financial transactions but also anything else that involves value-transfer such as voting or registering land ownership! Furthermore, you don't need any central authority to run a blockchain: they are essentially 'trustless' meaning that users can transact directly with each other without the need for any kind of financial intermediary.

A blockchain ledger itself is made up of a series of data sets (or blocks), which are linked and secured using cryptography. Each block contains batches of valid transactions that have been collected into 'blocks', which contain every transaction ever processed on the network since its creation. These blocks will all be verified by miners at some point in time, appended to the chain and then added to bitcoin's global public ledger called the 'blockchain'. New blocks are added to the bitcoin blockchain roughly every 10 minutes by miners who verify new transactions coming from users sending bitcoin between themselves. You can think of this as an open-source, distributed equivalent to conventional digital databases such as oracle or SQL server that can be used to store data about any type of asset, property or record.

So how do you know if a transaction actually occurred? There are several rules in place, which give us, confidence that the blockchain will not contain false information. Firstly, users must consent to their transactions by digitally signing them before broadcasting them over the network. Secondly, each block contains a timestamp, which is also signed and then appended to previous blocks when successfully verified by miners. Thirdly, all users on the network need to reach a consensus after verifying these few rules every time a new valid block is created; this is why we don't see forks (different chains) appearing from different mining companies due to conflicting information on when transactions were verified.

Finally, there is another layer of authentication present in the blockchain whereby every block contains a cryptographic hash of the previous one. Hashes are unique strings of numbers and letters that can only be created by hashing (encrypting) data using a seed value as input. This ensures that each new block will always contain the hash of the last one thus forming an unbroken chain, which will forever link and verify all these blocks together into one unified ledger! And if you're still not sure where this is going then let's assume that I'm buying a $10,000 house from you on your property over at 123 Main St, Anytown USA! Here's how we would do this: You have to transfer ownership rights for your house from yourself to me. This is essentially what happens when you send bitcoin over the blockchain and it costs a small amount of bitcoin in transaction fees for doing so. You would then transfer your house deed to an electronic smart contract on the blockchain, which can be easily verified by everyone else at minimal cost or effort. I, as a buyer, would now have all documentation necessary in order to prove that this transaction ever occurred (the signed contract) along with proof that every other person on the network has also seen it! (The smart contracts themselves are built securely using software logic and data stored on the blockchain.) Meanwhile, we'll both decide if there's any additional information we'd like to store electronically – maybe recording how much I paid for it after 5? Years (if you agree to wait that long for me to pay off the mortgage) – or we'll just leave it at a basic house transfer document.

Once 5 years have passed, if I haven't actually completed paying off your $10,000 mortgage on your home, then everyone can see how much time of ownership has elapsed and thus how much I still owe you after that period! But what if someone wants to hack the data? Well, due to its decentralized nature and use of cryptographic encryption, public blockchains like bitcoin's are designed in such a way that an attacker cannot change past records because doing so would alter all subsequent blocks after them. This means someone can virtually guarantee that their transaction occurred at the very moment they say it did. And most of the time, users will receive transaction notifications practically instantaneously!

This also means that we can develop other applications that depend upon the blockchain's immutability and use it for far more than just recording bitcoin transactions; smart property systems are already being developed in conjunction with ethereum-based smart contracts, which are essentially pieces of code that execute automatically when a certain condition is met. These systems would allow you to record who owns what property at all times and even provide various services such as paying your mortgage or distributing dividends based on how much “stock” someone has in a company. We'll talk about this more later! Ultimately, though, blockchains have to be trustworthy: they have to display integrity over time if users are to trust them. For this reason, most public blockchains are built with a schedule of planned upgrades called hard forks. These take place at precise times and require that network users upgrade their software to the new version or else they will no longer be part of the blockchain (aka “get left behind”).

Lastly, it's worth noting that blockchain technology will only improve with time. You'd be wise to keep an eye on developments in this technology and we'll certainly discuss the various changes here as they occur!

3

CRYPTOGRAPHY & BLOCKCHAIN SECURITY

What is Cryptography?

Cryptography is a form of art and science, which aims to provide secure communication in the presence of third parties. In our case, this means that we want to make sure others can't see what messages are being exchanged between you and me while still making it easy for both of us to verify each other's identities! We do this by creating systems ("algorithms") for encrypting data so that only those with proper authorization can read and decrypt them.

Cryptography is the science of secure communication in the presence of third parties (i.e. "adversaries") and for this reason; cryptography is also commonly referred to as cryptology.

Cryptography is used on all levels of human society, from military communications to transactions with cryptocurrencies. Cryptography provides security services such as confidentiality, integrity, authentication and non-repudiation.

In modern times, cryptography has been used extensively throughout all walks of life, from securing credit card purchases to protecting military secrets. In fact, most people use cryptographic algorithms every day without even knowing about it – just look at your browser! Here's another way in which blockchain technology is based on a solid foundation: it makes use of cryptographic algorithms to ensure that information is secure!

This chapter will cover some of the key cryptography concepts and how it is used on the blockchain, starting firstly with a brief overview of symmetric-key vs. public/private key encryption.

Cryptography 101

Symmetric-Key Cryptography:

This is the oldest type of encryption and is also known as "secret-key" or single-key cryptography. It involves using a single key for both encryption and decryption of data, which means that theoretically anyone who has access to this key can intercept and decrypt the message. The advantage of this method over others is that it requires less processing power and is simpler to implement. Symmetric-key ciphers are generally used when speed, efficiency and simplicity are valued over security; however, many experts feel that they are still safe against a determined adversary (for example symmetric AES 256 should be secure if implemented correctly). The main uses for these types of ciphers include file encryption, message encryption, authentication and hashing.

The most popular symmetric ciphers today are:

Asymmetric-Key Cryptography:

This is the newest type of encryption method and is also known as public-key cryptography. Public-key cryptography involves having two keys - a public key (which can be distributed to people who wish to send you secure messages) and a private key (which must never be shared or distributed). This infographic gives an overview of how it works; although it's slightly more complicated than this in practice:

How Assets Are Secured on The Blockchain Using Cryptographic Hashes And Elliptic Curve Cryptography (ECC): If we break down the process for storing assets on blockchain into simple steps, let's say you wanted to store a message on the Bitcoin blockchain:

Now we can use ECC cryptography to digitally sign our message using our private key (just like how we would sign a transaction with our wallet). This will give us our digital signature. Next, we can convert this message into binary format and then take the SHA-256 hash of it. This is known as hashing and it helps protect against data tampering. Finally, we tack on our digital signature before posting all of this information onto the Bitcoin network by packaging up everything in an OP_RETURN output that contains metadata about who wrote the message and when they did so. If anyone wants to read your message later on, they simply need to decode it using your public;) key to retrieve your digital signature and then hash it using SHA-256.

If the hashes match, then it means that there hasn't been any tampering and your message was written by you, otherwise, if they don't match then someone has tampered with the data. This helps protect against data tampering because since your digital signature is tied to a specific hash value for the original data (which is stored on Bitcoin's blockchain) anyone can verify that the message was written by you at a certain time.

Public/Private Key Cryptography vs. Symmetric-Key Cryptography: If we compare public/private key cryptography to symmetric-key cryptography we can see that they each have their own advantages and disadvantages.

For example, here is how some of these features stack up against each other:

Symmetric-Key Cryptography Public-Private Key Encryption Decryption with the same key used for encryption only allow one party to decrypt data (sender) must be able to encrypt and decrypt messages (sender & receiver) does not require advanced mathematical knowledge requires computational power allows only limited use cases such as message encryption and hashing requires the user to manually encrypt/decrypt messages can be used for digital signing allows for pseudonymous transactions

So Is Public-Private Key Cryptography Really Safer Than Symmetric-Key Cryptography?

A basic understanding of cryptography suggests that public-private key cryptography should theoretically be safer, but the answer isn't as straightforward as it seems; if we compare the two methods using the analogy of a door lock system then symmetric keys would be like having one master key that everyone has access to (which means you have to trust everyone else not to steal your stuff):

Symmetric Keys: *** *** In this analogy public-key cryptography would be like having two different types of locks on your front door - one a pin-and-tumbler type lock, and the other a combination lock. The locks are operated independently from each other - you can unlock your door by using one or the other of the locks. To do so, however, you must have some way of matching up the two types of keys to open each individual type. In order for this analogy to work perfectly in describing public key cryptography we would also need to assume that both locks were actually designed with different keys which could be used interchangeably (something they are not in reality). This just goes to show how much more complicated the real world is than an analogy and should help us keep things in perspective as we continue.

Cryptography Challenges

In order for public-key cryptography to work, there are a few challenges that must be overcome.

An Example of Problems that Public Key Cryptography Would Try to Solve:

Let's say we have two individuals, Alice and Bob. Both Alice and Bob have books they want to share with each other but don't want others in the world reading along. The obvious solution would be for them to take turns reading their books aloud to each other while sitting at opposite ends of a long hallway so that no one else can hear what they're saying. Assuming only these two people exist in the world this is perfectly safe - even if someone walked down the hall the noise from either end would drown out any attempts at listening in on their conversation or reading what was written on their books.

This is where we introduce Eve, the eavesdropper. Even if Alice and Bob sit at opposite ends of the earth in separate soundproofed rooms Eve can record their conversation or read what's on their book simply by listening into one end of the hall from another room far away. If Eve had perfect hearing, she may be able to listen through walls but let's assume that she does not have this ability. Instead, any information Eve gets by attempting to listen in on either Alice or Bob will be a garbled mess because they are sitting so far apart. This means that even if she spends her whole life trying to decipher who said what while ignoring everything else around her, it would still take longer than the lifetime of the universe to do so.

However, let's say that Alice and Bob each have an individual ability to make their voices louder or softer at will, but not completely mute themselves. If Alice wants to talk about a book, she read one week ago she simply lowers her voice by 10% when talking with Bob in order for him to hear her plainly. Now instead of the message being garbled beyond comprehension by Eve, it is clear enough for her to get some idea as what was discussed between them, without having any ability herself to read the information on either of their books. This change has accomplished two things - firstly, it takes away all advantages that Eve had regarding eavesdropping because now the sound from both ends of the hall can be heard equally. Secondly, the change also makes it harder for Alice and Bob to decipher what information was transmitted. It's all still there but each time one of them lowers their voice they simultaneously make it even more garbled and harder to hear by a 3rd party who doesn't know that it is possible to adjust volume like this.

Now add one more character into the mix - Charlie wants to listen in on conversations taking place between Alice and Bob without being detected by either of them, and he has an advanced machine that can 100% perfectly record everything said with perfect clarity whether it is whispered or shouted out loud. He first attempts using Eve's tactic of listening from a room far away but finds just like in real life his results are nothing but garbled noise. He then figures out that if he sits in the room with Alice or Bob he'll be able to hear everything they say just as it is being said, and thus has no problem recording both sides of a conversation at once.

Problem Solved? Not Yet!

This is where public-key cryptography comes in with its answer - when we say that this solution "solves" the eavesdropping problem what we really mean is that we have invented a system for Alice and Bob to talk to each other privately while preventing others from listening to them. The first thing you may notice about this statement is that it says nothing about stopping

Charlie from listening in on conversations between Alice and Bob using his advanced machine. There are tons of ways to stop him from doing that - he could simply be forced by law to not record the conversation, and laws are easy enough to break. He could also be forced not to copy the file he records without Alice or Bob's permission (or even more ridiculous - not allowed to replay it at all). His advanced machine may be stolen, destroyed, forcibly taken apart etc. There is no way for such a system of encryption combined with unbreakable cryptography alone to stop people like Charlie from recording private conversations in some way or another. It might seem like this is a huge flaw but it isn't. Nearly every cryptographic protocol out there can be broken by someone who knows what they're doing; yet despite their flaws we still use them on a daily basis because they are better than nothing at preventing eavesdropping.

To demonstrate this, let's look at a simplified example:

The Simplest Encryption Scheme in Existence

Alice has some secret that she wants to keep hidden from everyone else, so she comes up with a simple way of obscuring it that anyone can use: she just runs her message through an exclusive-or (XOR) operation which takes each letter and swaps it for the one directly on the right. For example: "Let them eat cake" would be encrypted like this - {"L", "e", "t", " ", etc.} then back again to get their plaintext version of the message. She then sends it out over telephone lines or any other unsecured medium. Bob, a bad man who wants to read her message but doesn't have access to the plaintext version herself, decides he'd like to steal it from her communications and so he starts eavesdropping on them. Eventually, Alice begins transmitting her secret: "Let them eat cake." What kind of person are you? Are you someone who would sit back and listen in peace knowing full well that because of how simple this encryption scheme is, even if you didn't hear the entire thing at least you know that most likely what was said wasn't anything terribly important or sensitive? Or do you want to be more proactive about privacy by getting all up inside other people's business with the advanced machine-based on some crazy piece of technology you invented yourself?

Blockchain Uses Cryptographic Hash Functions

A hash function is an algorithm for turning any piece of data into a unique, fixed-length output. The thing about hashing functions is that they are easy to calculate but incredibly difficult (nearly impossible) to reverse. Instead, you must go through the same exact process and have every bit of input match perfectly or else your output will not be correct. This allows us to very easily verify that our transaction records haven't been altered in any way when we compare hash values before and after a blockchain update! Let's look at how this works by examining two popular blockchains in more detail: bitcoin and ethereum.

Cryptography in Bitcoin: Hash Functions and Public Key Signatures

Bitcoin is built on a technology called blockchain, which allows users to trade digital “tokens” of value (aka bitcoins) with one another without the need for any middlemen. Instead, transactions are recorded in blocks that are chained together using something called a cryptographic hash function. This is why you'll often hear people refer to blockchains as secured by cryptography! There's no real magic about these hash functions; it's all just math. For example, let's say I tell you that two plus two equals four. It doesn't matter if I'm saying this now, or I said it last year when we were hanging out at my house - either way, you know that I'm right and two plus two equals four! It's math.

Bitcoin uses a cryptographic hash function known as SHA-256, which takes any input (a transaction or block of transactions) and computes the output (the “hash value”). The process is repeated thousands of times by different networks around the world to ensure that there is no tampering with data. This is called mining. Even though it sounds easy enough to do this in your bedroom, the truth is that billions upon billions of hashes are run per second on super computers, which were built just for this purpose, and yes they're still profiting handsomely from their investments! Nevertheless, if someone were to somehow change even just one number somewhere, the new hash value will not match up with all of these values (hashes) and thus can be detected.

Cryptography in Ethereum: Private and Public Key Pairs

Cryptography is also used extensively in the popular cryptocurrency ethereum. Blocks of transactions called smart contracts are created by a distributed global network of computers. These blocks have to contain the right information for them to be verified on the blockchain, which means that every transaction must include: The sender's public key (a unique identifier number) The recipient's public key (a unique identifier number) A value amount (in this case, ether tokens which act as ownership documents). Once any transaction is verified and added onto the chain, it can never be changed or removed - if someone were to try modifying their own transaction history or another person's they would immediately get caught. So how does this work exactly?

Cryptography makes use of two very different keys to identify and protect information: a public key and a private key. A bitcoin or ethereum address is 256 bits long. The first 80 bytes are used for the identification of your account - this part is public known as your address. If you're using it to check out someone else's transactions, then great! But if you're sending money from an exchange straight into your wallet, then you'll need to create a transaction that sends all of your balance (minus fees) to another person/address's account number; in order to do this there must be TWO things present: Your unique identifier (public key) Their unique identifier (public key) And please note here that I said PUBLIC keys, not the numbers themselves! Why is this? Well, it's because all of these values are used as "hashes" to generate a 256-bit string.

To create your public key, you use your private key - which is kept hidden and safe in your wallet - to multiply random bytes together (SHA-3) until you arrive at a 256-bit value. For example, if I told you that: The SHA-256 hash of ABCD1234 was 58298 then you would probably assume that my bitcoin address was ABCD1234, right? But instead, we have: The SHA-256 hash of 58298 was 1278928119650...etc. This is how we know that our account address is NOT the number itself! Now, let's say someone wanted to send you money. How would they do this? Well, I guess it depends on what kind of encryption your wallet uses. But in bitcoin your public key is actually hashed again with a SHA-256 hash function - THIS time however there are two slight changes: The first byte of the input (58298) is replaced by another random value. This ensures that no one can recreate your hashes without knowing both of these values!

Here's how it works: Let's assume my account address is ABCD1234: The person wanting to pay me sends over their unique identifier (public key) + the random number that we used earlier 5280 which comes out as 5620. This means that the actual public address (and therefore public key) of this transaction is: 5BDF1640CDD3431C993D0ABCD1234...etc. I now know that they want to send me money, so I can then add their new transaction into my own blockchain ledger. A few seconds later, once the network has verified and added their payment onto the chain, a hash - or string of letters and numbers - is generated; which can be used as a unique identifier for this transaction forever more :) For example: The SHA-256 hash of 5620 was D7A8BD50EB79061F5AC87ED2FB953288...etc. Now because we have changed our first byte of the input (the public key) we can see that it would be impossible for someone to send us money and spoof their address without knowing this new byte combination. Likewise, if you wanted to verify a transaction then all you'd have to do is hash it with SHA-256 again and compare the result with the transactions ID on the chain!

So now we know how to take a number and turn it into a string of random letters, numbers and symbols. But why is this useful? Well, you might be wondering about the second dotted line in the diagram above. Well, this is where you can use your public key - and therefore identify yourself - as an encryption key! Remember when I said earlier that if someone tried to modify their own transaction history or another person's they'd get caught because it would be immediately obvious by looking at the transactions ID? Well wouldn't it also make sense that whoever wanted to check up on this transaction would need both keys? And that if one of those keys was changed then again it would become apparent? Exactly! So, these two pieces of information can be used to create a high level of trust in your payments and blockchain!

So now that we understand the blockchain and how it works, let's talk about Ethereum...

What is ethereum?

Ethereum is an open platform that runs smart contracts: applications that run exactly as programmed without any possibility of downtime, censorship or third-party interference. These apps run on a custom built blockchain called 'etherum'.

You can build apps on top of ethereum using tools such as mist. Etherum' because their code is deterministic (i.e. if you put in certain inputs then you will always get out certain outputs). This contrasts to Bitcoin where the hashrate is controlled by SHA-256, which means there are a huge amount of possible outputs (e.g. 1 in 10 49).

For example, if I wanted to send you 0.5 ETH from my account address of '0x92A9Bafc008193E650a884f82287Ab215bC23775' then I would need to know your public key (or account address) and the amount that you would like to receive - i.e.:

Key: 0x92A9Bafc008193E650a884f82287Ab215bC23775
Value: 0x? Amount: 0.5

Input 1: value = 0x? input 2: public key =
QmRXvaVowjEy1fzgWVNQYnur1Pzy4C6FfxM

Receiver Address:
0x485A2C7B8047BAc8d312e33760db9b0a154A3513
Transaction

Hash:
032D814FC66649562572CD6AF5E0EEACB11FD593068B3FC
DA57F75E0883210D

Now, I know that the node stores the balance of all accounts on the machine (i.e. my private key is stored somewhere in memory); I can simply take any one of those addresses and send coins to it! This means that if you wanted to write an automated transaction paying multiple people, all you'd have to do is take their addresses and plug them into your script!

4

How Crypto Exchanges Work

What is a Cryptography Exchange?

These companies are where you can buy and sell cryptocurrencies, so they're essentially the "eBay" of cryptocurrency.

What's an exchange wallet?

The exchange will give you a digital address that's linked to your account; all your transactions will take place from this address. Make sure you don't expose this information anywhere (especially online) as someone could easily take your funds.

One of the most important things to consider when buying cryptocurrencies is security; if you keep all of your investments on an exchange, they're at risk from hackers/unscrupulous individuals who would rather just steal money than earn it legitimately. I'm not saying don't use exchanges but instead make sure you've got a backup plan in case your account gets hacked.

There are several different exchanges but I've used Poloniex and Bittrex so far; they both have their upsides and downsides -

if you want to read more about these go ahead and Google them, there's plenty of information available.

Firstly, I should mention the recent crypto exchange scams. This is largely where what seems to be a mainstream national exchange operator, usually outside of USA/western countries disappears with their customer's cryptocurrency. This is more common than you think and you should be careful which exchanges you use. You should always do your research.

What type of exchange should you use?

Well really it depends what country you're from but chances are that Coinbase will be your best bet if you're in the US (and even then, I don't see why you wouldn't want to use an exchange that had lower fees and a wider range of altcoins/cryptocurrencies). It's up to you whether or not you want to use an online wallet like Coinbase or something more secure like hardware or paper wallets - only store money on an online device that can access the internet. Always check for negative reviews before using any platform, as there are many exchanges out there that take advantage of naïve people

CryptoCurrency Exchanges: What Is Their Role?

There are many different cryptocurrency exchanges out there and in order for you to understand what they really do, its best we look at each of them individually.

Cryptocurrency exchanges came into existence because of a need to exchange one currency for another as well as provide price stability that everyone can count on.

In order to understand how crypto currency exchanges work, it's best to see what they do and how they accomplish their tasks. In essence, crypto currency exchanges are exactly like stock markets except with Bitcoin instead of dollars and at much higher rates - this means it's a lot easier to make a profit if you're willing to take risks. If you've ever wanted to trade currencies but don't have access to foreign money markets then it's possible to use crypto currency exchanges to get your hands on the currency you want.

The main role of crypto currency exchanges is to allow customers who have one form of cryptocurrency to buy another as well as provide a platform for buyers and sellers to meet.

There are many different types of exchanges but most of them operate in much the same way - they give you access to their system; let you deposit funds (and even credit cards) and then you place trades using an interface that they provide. This is how cryptocurrency exchanges stay in business; by providing users with a centralised location at which clients can make transactions from all over the world. The "middle-man" concept here is important because if someone wanted to trade with you face-to-face then they'd need to have your money with them - which wouldn't be very practical. The only disadvantage is that there needs to be a trust relationship between the buyer and seller; this means that someone could trade their BTC for USD (crypto-to-crypto) but when withdrawing then BTC might not be available at the same price so it's up to you to decide if this is within your risk threshold.

How Crypto Exchanges Operate

Here's our story. So, Alice wants to buy Bob some ETH on the Radex Exchange and sends her money from her Coinbase account over to the exchange. Once received, it is placed into a system called 'cold storage'. Cold storage is where you store your assets offline in order to prevent any hackers getting hold of them (i.e. they aren't connected to the internet). This means that if someone wanted try and steal Bob's money then they'd have no way of accessing it because their servers are disconnected from the blockchain! After 1-2 hours - when both their off-chain transactions have cleared - Alice's funds will appear in Bob's withdrawal address, which he can use as his proof of receipt for logging purposes! The same works for Bob who deposits his ETH from his wallet to Radex. After 1-2 hours the funds are verified and allow him to place buy and sell orders on the exchange!

Finally, here's a simple illustration how crypto exchanges work:

Let's go back to our employee example. Alice is an entry-level programmer working for Bob (who we've met before) at a company called 'BobCo'. She wrote her first line of code when she was 12 years old but was never taught how to write code that had any value so since then she has spent all her time learning how to write codes that can do stuff...even if it's only basic household chores!

Now that she's starting to learn how to write some valuable codes, we'll give her a bit of ETH so she can test out the network. She hears about this exchange called Radex and decides to try it out. Bob told her that there are already a lot of people on the platform, but nobody is really doing anything yet (which makes her nervous). Once logged in, she finds a nice-looking trading bot that looks great for beginners like herself - it only has one order type, which means all you have to do is enter the amount you want to buy or sell into its interface! It also takes care of placing an order and pushing it onto the blockchain for you! All you then need to do is wait patiently until your funds arrive at the exchange so you can trade it!

Crypto Exchanges are really just like any traditional exchange. You have your buyers and sellers (i.e., traders). Traders are people who place buy or sell orders for other users to match with them! These orders are then placed into an order book which is a list of all the buy and sell orders available on the exchange that will be executed as soon as someone finds a matching order in the opposite direction (i.e., you want X amount of ETH but only Y amounts are available - when you match with another investor, they'll send their portion over to you!). Order books can be thought of like Google Sheets; it's a long sheet separated into columns so multiple people can write down what they'd like to trade (i.e. A = 100 ETH, B = 50, etc.). The sheet is then separated into rows that are filled with the most popular trades people have been exchanging in (i.e. A: 100 ETH, B: 100 ETC, C: 10 LTC...). Crypto exchanges work the same way except all of your trades are placed on a public ledger so everyone can see for themselves! Your order will stay on the book until another investor finds an order matching yours and they will execute it automatically for you!

After hearing about this new exchange, Bob wants to give it a go too! He also has some ETH he's looking to trade so he logs out of his Coinbase wallet and over onto Radex. After signing up for an account he deposits some funds into his new exchange wallet and fires up the trading bot he set up. The interface is a lot easier to use than what Alice was experiencing so he decides to trade in some of his ETH for some ETC!

The process will work exactly like it did before with Bob: As soon as he places an order, it gets pushed onto the network where Matica will verify that all of its funds are real. After 1-2 hours, you'll find your fund in your withdrawal address allowing you to send them from Radex back onto Coinbase. Now that both Alice and Bob have gone through their trading experience, they're not going anywhere without making sure it wasn't a fluke - right? We decided we should check out crypto exchanges

The Technology of Crypto Exchanges

The exchanges are also run on 'Blockchain'. As mentioned previously, this technology is responsible for recording every transaction made in the exchange. Each trade done on the exchange creates its own block and gets added to a public ledger that everyone can see - this is what makes them so secure!

A 'smart contract' is like an automated record bookkeeper. It watches you place orders in the book it's working with and finds compatible orders filled by other traders. They are then sent over to either match or automatically execute your order without any human involvement (which saves these companies money)!

Crypto Exchanges work using something called a REST API. In short, they allow one website to send information to another (like how Google Sheets can send data directly into an excel sheet). The other exchange will then post the matching order and automatically execute it for you, saving you time!

This technology is also used by companies like Google to allow them to sync data between their offices. If they want an engineer in San Jose to know what's going on with a customer in Nevada, all they need to do is stream that information over using this technology. The engineer can see the changes made in real-time without having to wait until he gets back into the office!

Accessing Your Funds

Many new users are worried with how exchanges store your funds when you choose to trade through them. In truth, most of these services use public ledgers, which means all transactions, are public knowledge - meaning there aren't many surprises when it comes to accessing your funds. For example, let's say you're currently trading through an exchange that you deposited 100 ETH into (which is worth $40,000 right now). You decide to trade your ETH for ETC, which would then give you 30 ETC, and 70 ETH after the transaction - resulting in a total of 130ETH ($56,000). The order book will show that someone has opened up an order looking to trade 70ETH for 1000 ETC at market price - they've also added a fee onto the top saying they'll pay a 5% withdraw fee if anyone wants to access their newly acquired ETC. Someone else on the other hand will look over your order and determine that it's a smart move for them to make based on the amount you're willing to pay - they'll claim it and you'll almost instantly have access to your ETC!

If you plan on trading cryptocurrencies then having an idea of what the technology behind it all is: Blockchain, Smart Contracts & REST APIs like Google Sheets. We can note that cryptocurrency exchanges are also using this technology behind the scenes but they're not typically changing anything about them. At their core, these technologies are used exactly how they were intended and work in a way that many people would assume already does (like Google sheets).

In summary, crypto exchanges are a place for users to trade cryptocurrencies. It's important to understand these differences if you're planning on trading because it will allow you to have a better understanding of how the technology behind crypto exchanges works!

5

Why Crypto Markets Fluctuate So Rapidly?

Why Crypto Markets Fluctuate So Rapidly?

These companies are where you can buy and sell cryptocurrencies, so they're essentially the "eBay" of cryptocurrency.

The first thing that needs to be explained is why Bitcoin and other cryptocurrencies are swing like crazy. During times of market volatility, traders will try and 'buy low' (let's say BTC is $2,500) then once it goes up for them they'll start selling off their coins for a profit - this is called profit-taking. This in turn causes a vacuum that sucks all other BTC value up and pushes the price to $3,000 - which then forces another trader to buy low and sell high until they've managed to take their profits off the table. In cryptocurrency trading we call this 'market manipulation'.

In some ways, it isn't too different from how stock markets operate however there are also many differences. For example, dollar values in crypto currency markets fluctuate at a much higher rate because of market manipulation (no one can say for sure what would happen if the same amount of money was being used). Another reason why we see huge swings is due to a lack of general understanding on how currencies move - which means people are always predicting market movements without fully understanding why they're moving the way they are.

In summary, it's important to understand that markets swing for many reasons but mostly because of market manipulation and psychological game playing. The crypto currency community is still young and full of first-time traders - it will take some time before we see less volatility.

6

How To Win At Crypto Currency Trading?

How To Win at Crypto Currency Trading?

The short answer: Yes! The longer answer is: It's possible if you have enough money to make a lot of trades at once or wait patiently for the price point, you're looking for to arrive over time (this method allows you to ride out any bear trends in order to get the cheapest coins possible).

The short answer: Yes! The longer answer is: It's possible if you have enough money to make a lot of trades at once or wait patiently for the price point, you're looking for to arrive over time (this method allows you to ride out any bear trends in order to get the cheapest coins possible).

The longer answer is a little bit more difficult to understand. The easiest way for someone to win at crypto currency trading is by knowing what they are doing; this means having full control over their emotions and being able to think clearly when making decisions. People tend to do very well when they focus on only one thing, especially if that thing is relevant to the career or interest that they're in.

In summary, it's possible for you to win at crypto currency trading if you have enough money (multiple accounts), patience & have basic knowledge about: psychology, game theory & how markets work.

You should also ask yourself some questions before jumping into something like this such as "do I really want to make these kinds of decisions or am I in this for the money?"

To win at crypto trading you need three things: Time, Money and Knowledge. You will also have to be willing to pick up new skills along the way that can help you get what you're ultimately looking for in the end!

Are There Any Good Ways to Make Profit from Crypto Currency Markets?

This is something a lot of people are asking themselves, especially if they're just starting out and hoping for profit immediately. The easiest way I've found over the years is by day trading (you can make sizeable amounts of money with this method these days given the popularity of crypto but it's not as profitable as it used to be). In order to do this effectively you'll need a strong understanding of behavioural economics and human psychology because after all these are markets driven by people who can be manipulated.

The most important thing you can do to better your chances of profiting in crypto trading is to educate yourself and get to know as many people as possible who are investing into similar fields (the more knowledge the better). If I were to tell you that this would be easy, then I'd be lying because it takes a lot of time; especially if you want to fully understand how these markets work. It's difficult but not impossible!

7

Bitcoin Trading And Investing Strategies

Bitcoin Trading and Investing Strategies

These are mainly the same thing but let's admit it, this is a lot more fun. Trading strategies for Bitcoin are different to those that you would use in stocks because of numerous factors such as speed (how fast things move in crypto markets) and market volatility.

Trade more than the average person: It's a lot easier to make money in cryptocurrency trading when you take the approach of trading more coins compared to the average trader (if they're only interested in making money by flipping a coin). As previously mentioned, this means that it will require much less skill as all you need to do is find coins that are likely to increase in value over time and hold onto them. [Better at picking coins = Easier]

The amount of trades isn't really important - but how many transactions you can make based on your investments. You shouldn't be focusing on how much profit you're going to gain from these trades but instead focus on increasing your portfolio size. Later, we'll talk about some methods of trading that require a certain amount of coins in order to make money.

Trade with your favourite coin: The easiest way to trade Bitcoin is simply by holding onto it and waiting for the value to increase over time. In other words, this means waiting until the price increases (see Chapter 2).

It's also worth noting that you shouldn't be too worried about how much profit you're going to receive on each trade because it's the overall profit that will determine if all of your trades paid off - not just one If you went 'all in' with Ripple at $0.15 and sold at $2.50 - Your return would be 3,250% ($0.21 per Ripple x 100 = 21).

<u>5 key strategic methods for crypto investing and trading that will make it a lot easier to get the results you desire:</u>

1. Buy Low, Sell High (Traditional method)
2. Start off with only 1 or 2 coins (reduce risk and don't chase after multiple coins at once or risk over-trading/negative emotions) - then add later if you're confident enough & they fit your portfolio. Example: "if your coin is up 500% and you have no sell order in place, chances are you'll end up taking this profit due to greed"
3. Use all of your money when starting out (Don't rely on getting more money soon) - If you use all of your capital, there's nothing to lose - so do your research and use common sense when picking coins.
4. Monitor multiple markets (especially the 24-hour volume because it's a lot quicker than most regulated exchanges). It's possible to make money from both trading & holding at the same time - although this is quite

difficult so it's best to focus on only one of these methods per coin.

5. If you're going to hold onto a coin for longer periods of time, don't worry about using an exchange that's more suitable for short-term trades or bigger volumes (although there are some popular coins worth holding in order to make large profits).

Tip: When looking to trade between $1-$10 it can be useful to take advantage of Bittrex which has lower fees associated with this.

When to buy and sell coins: The most important thing to consider when trading cryptocurrencies is pricing, volume, exchanges/markets and news (such as Bitcoin forks). If you're holding onto specific coins for a longer period of time then it's best to hold them in a wallet that can be accessed at any time so that you never miss out on market opportunities. It's also worth noting that the majority of altcoins have no real purpose other than just being used as an alternative means of payment - even though there are some exceptions such as Ethereum and Ripple which have 'features' compared to just simply being used for payments.

8

ALTCOIN INVESTING & TRADING

What are Altcoins?

Altcoins are cryptocurrencies other than Bitcoin. An altcoin is just a fancy term for any cryptocurrency that isn't bitcoin. There were almost 9,000 altcoins in existence as of March 2021 and they all have different features so it's hard to tell which one will be the next big thing!

Altcoins are cryptocurrencies other than Bitcoin with some defining characteristics or properties like smart contracts or low-price volatility. Many who get involved quickly find themselves overwhelmed by how difficult each coin is unique from another on key aspects like price stability and market cap making it impossible to predict what might become popular next.

Altcoins are simply alternative cryptocurrencies to bitcoin, which are considered worth investing in, or at least holding onto for the longer term - there's a lot of features associated with Altcoins apart from just being used as another cryptocurrency. These features can be useful, such as smart contracts, but they may not necessarily be what people choose to use them for - even though it could make altcoin prices much higher.

Altcoin investing and trading summary

Although trading altcoins can be a lot of fun, it's not worth risking your own capital unless you know what you're doing (which is why this article exists). If you don't want to take my word for it, that's fine; however, keep in mind that there are plenty of people who do end up losing all of their capital by investing/trading in altcoins as they have no idea about what they're doing. The most important aspect when making attempts at turning a profit from an alternative coin is being able to identify market opportunities - which will come with experience and practice. It's also worth noting that if someone tells you something like "this coin is going to the moon" then chances are that it isn't.

Here are 11 key methods for creating a winning portfolio:

1. Invest in coins that have good projects/ideas behind them - If you're unsure about the idea then research the developers and make sure it makes sense for them to be doing what they're doing when considering their background & current employment situation. The more effort they've put into their coin, generally means that it's worth investing in (although there are exceptions). You can identify this by reading white papers, looking at roadmaps & reading forum posts (Reddit is one of the best resources).

2. Hold onto coins with low market caps whenever possible - although small market cap coins can sometimes die out completely, these are quite rare so it could be worth holding onto these coins for longer periods of time.

3. Make sure you're always updating your portfolio with the latest developments regarding each coin - this is an essential part of keeping track of which coins are worth investing in and which ones aren't.

4. Try to choose a few altcoins that fall into different categories (such as infrastructure, privacy etc.) so that there's less competition in any given market and therefore more potential profits.

5. Research & monitor trends before making purchases - if you're not confident enough or don't have enough money to invest, then it might be best to avoid making purchases at all costs.

6. If something sounds too good to be true, then it probably is - no one knows how high/low a coin will go, so it's best to stay on the safe side and avoid being scammed.

7. Google everything - this may sound obvious but there have been a lot of coins that I've invested in which have turned out to be scams/ponzi schemes etc., and they're usually quite easy to spot if you know what you're doing (researching will help with this).

8. Only invest what you can afford to lose - no matter how nice someone is or how much proof they give you of their claims, don't invest anything that you won't be able to live without.

9. Don't believe anyone who says crypto isn't risky - This article has tons of information about how risky cryptocurrency trading can potentially be and although it's possible to make money from it, you also run the risk of losing (this goes for everything in life). It's risky because there are things like wallet hacking and other scams that can cost people thousands or even millions.

10. Don't invest more than you're willing to lose - this is something that I've said before but will reiterate here as it seems to be one of the most commonly overlooked pieces of advice when it comes to trading altcoins/cryptocurrency in general. Just because your

investment is small/worthless doesn't mean that you should gamble with it; if you don't understand something then do further research until you do. If investing in cryptocurrency makes you feel uncomfortable then avoid doing so at all costs - there's no point in losing mental (let alone real) wealth.

11. Don't listen to anyone who tells you how much a coin will go up/down by - no one knows what the price of anything is going to do, and by telling people that they "have to invest before it moons" then you're helping them make money off your naivety or greed; don't be fooled by these types of statements (the only way someone has any idea about the future price is if they have some insider information). Although nobody should be listening to anyone who's making predictions like this, there are likely many more people than you think that are falling for these tactics.

9

ETHEREUM

Ethereum

Ethereum is a platform that makes it possible for any developer to build and publish next-generation decentralized applications.

Ethereum can be used to develop applications that serve as a transparent, more democratic and efficient version of the services we use today like banking, crowd funding, or even Reddit. Some people have criticized Ethereum for its similarities with Bitcoin & called it a "Bitcoin clone"; it's been around since mid-2015 and has gained a lot of popularity over the last year. It should be noted that although it is still possible to create applications using Bitcoin's blockchain, Ethereum offers much more flexibility than its counterpart due to its Turing complete internal code and large development community.

This post will address some of the most common questions people have about Ethereum and hopefully provide some insight into what makes it the second-largest cryptocurrency.

Q. What is a Turing Complete language?

A. A Turing complete Language, as explained by the MIT Technology Review, is "any programming language in which a computable function can be expressed", meaning that unlike high-level languages like C++ or Java, it is impossible for a Turing complete language to have an algorithm where the potential output is not known.

There's also an additional rule with Turing Complete languages called "halting problem" which means that there can never be an algorithm or program created which will tell you if a given computation will ever stop running (this ties back into how Ethereum can run indefinitely)

Q. How do smart contracts work?

A. Smart contracts are a key part of what makes Ethereum so different from Bitcoin and other altcoins, they allow users to execute codes on the blockchain in exchange for monetary value/asset, such as if I were able to write an algorithm that paid you money every time you sent me a message on Twitter (this is an oversimplified example but it should help you get the basic idea of how smart contracts work).

The codes that are written for these contracts can be as specific or generalized as necessary, which means that they could be used for all sorts of uses: voting systems, decentralized autonomous organizations, governance systems, or even as a means of trade between two parties.

As you'll see in the next section, smart contracts are also non-reversible which is something that cannot be said about Bitcoin, however, there is no need to fret because Ethereum provides an audit trail (also known as 'modifiable computing'), which allows users to view transactions before they are completed.

Q. How do I use/buy Ethereum?

A. At the time of writing this article, there are 3 ways to purchase ether; through exchanges like Poloniex or Coinbase (more on these later) with fiat currency, buying it directly from people who already have it using a service like LocalEthereum, or mining them with a GPU or CPU.

Depending on which way you choose to acquire ether, there are different benefits associated with each method: if you mine it yourself you will obviously have more control over your coins and won't need to pay any fees; if you buy from an individual the benefit is that the cost of purchasing can be much less than purchasing it from an exchange, and if you buy through an exchange the benefit is that you have a much larger selection of coins to choose from (at the moment there are over 30 altcoins being traded on Poloniex).

Q. How do smart contracts work on Ethereum?

A. As discussed earlier, smart contracts are pieces of code that have a monetary value associated with them and run on the blockchain, so if you were to buy a smart contract from someone you would basically be buying that code (which could be anything).

Q. What does the blockchain look like?

A. Since there are many different types of transactions made every day, Ethereum's blockchain can become quite large and unwieldy over time; however, to facilitate users' experiences, they have implemented "sharding" which allows nodes on the blockchain to be split into smaller groups, allowing for quicker computations (also known as "virtual shards").

It should also be noted that there is a difference between Ethereum and Ethereum Classic, with the latter being an entirely separate blockchain that was created when Ethereum's pre-sale backer crowdfunds were hacked in 2016.

Q. What's the difference between proof of stake and proof of work?

A. Proof of stake is a newer consensus algorithm that was implemented on Ethereum after it had been breached several times; the basic idea behind PoS is that you lock up an amount of bitcoin (or ether) for X amount of time (a couple of weeks for example) which allows you to mine on the blockchain.

Q. How can I use Ethereum?

A. With a blockchain that is Turing complete, users are able to do literally anything with Ether (bitcoin's only constraint was whether or not the developers would go along with it). Users can create games, businesses, financial institutions, file storage, gambling sites, stock markets, prediction markets and much more.

If you plan on using Ethereum for any type of financial purpose you will need to use an ERC-20 compatible wallet.

Q. How do I purchase an altcoin? What's in the future for Ethereum/altcoins?

A. To purchase any type of altcoin you will need to first purchase bitcoin or ether, which can then be exchanged for an altcoin using an exchange like Poloniex. As far as the future of Ethereum/altcoins goes, that remains to be seen but there is no telling what may happen.

The important thing is not necessarily how, but why you're buying it.

If you're buying it to conduct transactions, then Ethereum may be the best option for you.

If you are buying it because of its advanced scripting language then Bitcoin has a much more extensive library.

Q. How can I read the blockchain?

A. The blockchain is public information, which means that anyone who wishes to view it can; however, the blockchain is over 300GB in size, which makes it very difficult to analyze.

The easiest way to view and understand information on a blockchain is to visit something like Etherscan, a site that has already done all of the work for you (although make sure to double-check everything).

Q. Why do developers use the Ethereum blockchain?

A. All blockchains essentially do the same thing, but developers choose to utilize Ethereum for a couple of reasons; first of all, it is very easy to interact with and write smart contracts on Ethereum and also because Ether has much broader use cases than bitcoin.

Q. How does mining work? What are miners incentivized by? How do they get paid?

A. Miners are incentivized by the block reward, which is currently 5 ether, and may increase or decrease based on how much demand there is from developers (the more demand, the higher the price of Ether).

The way mining works is that each miner runs a computer program that connects them to Ethereum's network; this program includes data on the block header (who sent how much to whom at what time) and a "nonce" which is a random number (usually a 32-digit hexadecimal string).

When run, miners are able to generate hashes that link the nonce with the information on the blockchain in a way that matches all of the previous blocks' algorithms; this link is called a "hash". Because each hash contains something from the block header, if it matches all of the pre-existing hashes then it is accepted by the network and miners receive their 5 ether as well as transaction fees.

This process typically takes 10 minutes (or longer) and is not very energy efficient.

Q. How is ether created?

A. Ether (the currency) is mined just like any other cryptocurrency; the only difference is that it has a pre-determined maximum supply of 100 million ether and block rewards are given out every 12 seconds instead of 50 or 25 coins per block as in Bitcoin's case.

Q. How do I use Ether?

A. Like any other cryptocurrency, you will need an ERC-20 compatible wallet to send and receive ether from others; MyEtherWallet is highly recommended for this purpose. You can also store your ether on exchanges like Poloniex or Bittrex just like most other cryptocurrencies but please, make sure to use 2FA every time you log in.

Q. What is a smart contract? Can you give an example?

A. A smart contract is essentially a computer program that runs on the Ethereum network; it contains information about how the program works and what actions are taken if certain conditions are met (certain action = transaction).

Propy is an example of a project that uses smart contracts to help you buy real estate: the program and transaction information are all stored on the blockchain, so no one can tamper with any of your data. The entire process is very transparent and public.

A typical ERC-20 token contract contains things like: start date, end date, initial supply, totalSupply (total number of coins), owner address and time (block).

Q. What are tokens?

A. Tokens are essentially applications that run on the Ethereum network; they are developed by an entity (company) in order to raise money for the project through ICOs, which is basically a process where you send Ether to the address of a smart contract in exchange for tokens.

Q. How can I invest in an ICO?

A. If you are able to send Ether from a wallet that supports ERC-20 contracts (one that has ETH), then you can invest by sending ether directly to the transaction signed address on websites such as Token Market, Icodrops or Coin Schedule.

Everyone should be extremely careful and make sure to do their research before making any investments; in fact, many people including myself would argue that ICOs are very risky.

Q. What is a DAPP?

A. The difference between a dapp and a DApp is simply that "dapp" is used to refer to an application or service while "Dapp" or "decentralized application" refers to the actual software that the dapp uses for storage, communication and so on.

Q. What is a token sale? Can you give an example?

A. A token sale (also referred to as ICO) is basically just like an IPO but instead of shares of stock you are receiving tokens of the project you are investing in. Token sales can be risky ventures but also highly profitable if research has been done and the project is legit.

A few examples of projects that did well after their token sale: Qtum, Iconomi, Augur, Golem, Basic Attention Token (BAT).

Q. What is an ERC-20 token?

A. An ERC-20 token is a type of Ethereum token protocol that conforms to the rules set forth by the Ethereum developers and allows for tokens to be sent from one address (wallet) to another within seconds instead of minutes or hours depending on network congestion.

Q. How do I exchange one cryptocurrency for another?

A. You can trade cryptocurrencies on exchanges like Poloniex or Bittrex; most of them have an option to use 2FA (2-factor authentication) for extra protection against hacks and scams. Please see the links above for further instructions and details about each exchange.

Q. What is airdrop? How can I participate?

A. Airdrops are events in which a particular cryptocurrency will distribute free tokens or coins to anyone who owns a certain amount or type of cryptocurrency (it's very similar to mining but instead of money they give away tokens). For example, if you are holding 1 BTC, then you may be eligible for an airdrop of 0.1 BTC depending on the rules that were set forth by a particular project.

Please see the links above for further instructions and details about each airdrop.

Q. What is Bitcoin? How does it work?

A. People often confuse Ethereum with Bitcoin (or BTC). While both projects are based on blockchain technology and share many similarities, they are two separate entities; in fact, Ethereum was actually created after people became uncomfortable with certain aspects of the Bitcoin network (i.e. lack of decentralized governance, costly transaction fees and slow confirmation times).

Q. Why is Ethereum different from other cryptocurrencies?

A. The main difference between Ethereum and many other cryptocurrencies is that it was designed to be a platform for applications to run on (similar to how the internet works); meaning that developers can build applications (apps network) on top of the Ethereum and have them run efficiently and securely without worrying about attacks or censorship from special interest groups.

Ethereum also has a more flexible programming language than Bitcoin-based projects, meaning that it is easier to build dapps without having to learn an entirely new coding language.

Q. What is Gas in Ethereum?

A. The network of nodes used to process transactions on the Ethereum blockchain are all connected through an internet connection and a mesh network; each node basically verifies every transaction that it receives by running them through its own code to make sure they are legitimate and then sends them along to the other nodes for verification.

To give the nodes an incentive to process and verify transactions, the Ethereum network requires users to pay a fee (in Gas) for each transaction they send out. The more complex or larger a particular transaction is, the more Gas it takes up; this means that gas acts as a way to limit how much users can do with their applications on the platform.

Q. What is Ethereum Classic and what caused the split from the core Ethereum network?

A. Following a hack on The DAO in 2016, an Ethereum project that allowed users to develop applications using smart contracts (similar to how Google lets you create apps for phones), many people called for a hard fork of the blockchain so that they could get their money back; since the core developers of Ethereum disagreed with this decision, a group of miners (who provide computing power to the network and are compensated for doing so) decided to fork off Ethereum from its original blockchain into the new "ethereum classic" chain.

Q. What is ICO (Initial Coin Offering)? How does it work?

A. There are a few different types of tokens that you will find on crypto exchanges; the most popular one is the coin, which is used to represent a certain cryptocurrency project (like Bitcoin and Litecoin). However, there are also other kinds of tokens such as asset-backed tokens or utility tokens.

Ethereum projects often create their own tokens to use on their platform; this is done through an ICO (Initial Coin Offering). During the ICO phase, developers will release a certain amount of coins and sell them to people who want to use that particular application. This means that if you are interested in a specific project, you can buy some of its tokens during the ICO stage before it goes live.

Q. What is a token and why do developers use them?

A. A "token" refers to a certain digital asset that you can use on a specific platform; when you purchase tokens from an ICO, it grants you access to the related service provided by the company (i.e. if you invest in XYZ's ICO, then you will have access to XYZ's social network service).

A token can also be used as a representation for something (i.e. a token may be worth $0.10 in the future if it holds $0.15 USD fiat value); this means that tokens are often traded on crypto exchanges and can act as investments if you believe that the service associated with a certain token will be used by lots of people in the future.

Q. What is BitconGold? How does it work?

A. Bitcoin Gold (aka BTG) is an alternative cryptocurrency to Bitcoin that allows miners to mine blocks faster and on a different blockchain; this means that if you own Bitcoin (BTC) you will also receive an equal amount of BTG if you hold BTC in a wallet at the time that BTG is created.

Q. Why are some ICOs banned in China?

A. Some countries, such as China and South Korea, have banned Initial Coin Offerings because they feel that it gives off the wrong impression to investors, and it can often lead to scams or pump-and-dump schemes.

Q. What is the "SkinCoin" token?

A. SkinCoin is a type of cryptocurrency that allows users to gamble on eSports games such as Dota2; you buy SKIN for fiat currency and use it to bet on matches in a similar manner to how you would bet with real money.

Q. What is an ICO (Initial Coin Offering) rating service? How does it work?

A. An ICO rating service is a platform that ranks different cryptocurrencies according to certain criteria that they believe define the quality of a project; one common type of ranking system uses a letter grade to indicate how "good" a certain ICO is.

Here are the key features of Etheruem:

1. Smart Contract
2. Decentralized Application
3. Computing platform
4. Peer to peer network
5. Consensus algorithm (Ethereum uses proof of work)

If you're thinking about getting into cryptocurrency, it's best to take slightly larger positions than normal are still plenty of people who are making lots of money via trading/investing it's only a matter of time until most of these experienced traders start moving their money into other markets. Things might change in the future when more people become involved with cryptocurrency investing but until then this is something you should be aware of.

Pick one or two coins that you think have the most potential for both short/mid-term gains and long-term gain (or at least have the potential for one of them) - personally, I like Ripple, Monero, and ZCash as they all have real world use cases which will help strengthen the crypto market in general long-term.

The Future of Cryptocurrency

There will always be new ICO's and crypto products being created - there is, however, currently an oversupply of these so people need to choose their investments carefully before purchasing; this means knowing everything possible about a given project before putting money down. I believe we'll see many more "pump and dump" schemes in 2018, which is why it's important for you to do your research thoroughly and not just rely on what someone else tells you (Google is your best friend).

10

Smart Contracts/Dapps

Smart Contracts/Dapps

Ethereum is a platform that makes it possible for any developer to build and publish next-generation decentralized applications.

Smart contracts are used to improve the overall efficiency of a given business, it can be anything from an audit trail for accounting purposes to storage of information for legal cases; the use cases are endless but there's still a lot of room for growth in this area.

Famous cryptocurrencies such as Ethereum have built-in support for smart contracts so they're also compatible with other programs and Dapps that you may come across while researching cryptocurrency-related topics.

The biggest problem facing smart contracts/Dapps is scalability - many people believe that full nodes could potentially play a part in improving the scaling issues associated with these two technologies (particularly when combined) but right now there isn't any real solution available. The fact that transaction costs are often quite high is also a bit of an issue as it could potentially scare potential buyers away from using smart contracts/Dapps; there are currently solutions such as Raiden Network which are attempting to remedy this situation, but there's no telling when these technologies will be fully implemented.

As smart contracts and Dapps evolve they will play a part in turning blockchain technology into something that revolutionizes many different industries over the next few years.

Key Smart Contract /Dapp Concepts

Smart contracts and Dapps are two different things but they work in the same sort of way.

The blockchain is what helps these technologies function properly (as blocks keep data secure) which means it's important for you to be familiar with the bitcoin blockchain when researching smart contracts/Dapps; I'll be covering this in more detail shortly so continue reading if you're interested. The most popular programming languages used for smart contracts and Dapps include Solidity, Serpent, LLL, Mutan and Viper - there are also ethereum specific tools that can make development faster such as truffle and web3js. You will find a lot of exchanges/marketplaces that only deal with cryptocurrency enabled by ethereum right now which is why it's important to know how these two products works; they are, in fact, complimentary products that need each other for survival.

The blockchain consists of blocks and these blocks are essentially data containers that store/link to previous blocks (this is what makes the chain so strong) - each block contains a timestamp, transaction information and a link to the previous "parent" block. The bitcoin blockchain is constantly growing because new transactions are added all the time; in order for this to take place there needs to be consensus which helps ensure that all nodes can agree on what has taken place at any given point in time (by using cryptographic evidence).

Ethereum's smart contracts are fairly complex computers/programs that run on top of ethereum's blockchain - they're not actually built into the network itself; as mentioned earlier, these contracts work with Dapps that can be built using any of the supported programming languages. For example, let's take a look at what bitcoin smart contracts look like (hint: they're not really that complex although some people believe that ethereum offers better functionality in this regard).

You should now have a basic understanding of how bitcoin smart contracts/Dapps work and you'll notice from the descriptions above that they actively interact with existing product(s) or service(s); this means I will be covering these products in detail below so continue reading if you're interested. A lot of business are actually just starting to realise the potential benefits of implementing one or more forms of blockchain technology into their operations but there aren't many specific examples available; it will probably a few years before blockchain based technologies start to become mainstream.

Deeper dive into Dapps/smart Contracts

Dapps are decentralized applications that run on top of a blockchain and smart contracts work closely with Dapps in the sense that they help govern/administer these products - they're not actually responsible for overseeing any sort of transactions though. It's important to remember that all of this data is public (or semi-public) which means businesses need to be careful when signing onto one or more Dapp(s); you should also keep in mind that users will be able to access these Dapps without having to go through an intermediary, like a web page or centralized server.

One way to think about it is by using eBay as an example; let's say I have some rare baseball cards that I want to sell online but there are multiple people who want to buy. I could use a centralized service like eBay because they hold my stuff for me and also help with payment (they take a small percentage of the sale price as well). The problem is that there's no way to regulate payments in this scenario; people can essentially cheat/steal or even send you fake money which means it opens up an entirely new set of security concerns for you to worry about.

If, on the other hand, I used eBay but had bitcoin smart contracts govern everything then only people who have money will be able to bid on my cards (because their money would need to exist within the blockchain) - that way if someone tried sending me fake money it wouldn't work because it has nothing backing it up. There's really no way to cheat in this scenario because it's all handled by the blockchain/bitcoin smart contracts; there is also a scarcity factor because my cards have been placed into the blockchain for everyone to see (you can't create fake ones). The only issue with this example is that everything would take place automatically so users might not even know who they're actually dealing with!

Another example: I could go on craigslist and rent out an apartment via smart contract for $800 USD / month but again, there's no way of knowing if the person paying me actually has any money - as soon as I hand over the keys they could just run off without paying me at all... unless smart contracts were used which would mean a digital deposit could be placed into the blockchain like a promissory note.

Now, there will always be people who are sceptical about these new technologies so let's take a look at some of the common concerns; you may have heard that smart contracts and Dapps might not actually work correctly all the time but that simply isn't the case - individuals (or companies) can build them to perform specific tasks which means they will never do anything outside of their programming mandate or function. In other words, it's impossible for ethereum smart contracts to destroy your files or steal your money.... if you program them to act rationally/logically then they will only do what they were programmed to do.

Another common concern is where security is concerned because I'm sure we've all heard about this before - there are many computer based systems that have been hacked in the past which means users may think it's a real issue but in reality, a blockchain like ethereum or bitcoin can never be hacked. This is because blockchains rely on decentralization which means no one person/entity has control over them; if someone wants to hack into your account and steal your money then they would need to break through multiple security measures (verification, encryption) and then reverse-engineer the protocol which just isn't possible for anyone to do at this time.

One key point people often forget about: you don't actually have to use a cryptocurrency when using smart contracts... any type of payment system will work. This means if you want to use a credit card or PayPal then that's absolutely fine because it will all be done via the blockchain. In fact, ethereum has recently began creating plans for an ERC-20 token standard which would allow anyone to create their own token/currency and place it into the blockchain for others to see; these tokens can also be traded exclusively on decentralised exchanges like Etherdelta (which is a smart contract itself).

The last thing I think about when trying to visualize how this new technology works is by thinking about genetics - life isn't possible without DNA so we might as well try looking at smart contracts in the same way. This analogy isn't perfect but let's just say that DNA (or bitcoin) is what makes everything possible and then smart contracts are actually the code, which helps guide/control these technologies; in other words, DNA is what allows users to interact with this technology while smart contracts tell bitcoin how it should behave.

There are many benefits to using blockchain technology but one of the biggest ones I keep hearing about is how it can be used for micro-transactions. For example, let's say you want to buy a domain name from someone but you only have $1 USD available so you would need to send that person 1 cent (or 100 satoshis). In reality, however, most people don't even know that much about cryptocurrencies so they wouldn't necessarily be able to handle something like that. That's where smart contracts come in because they can make micropayments extremely easy - this is just one example of how blockchains could be used.

With that said, the blockchain is still in its infancy stage and there's nothing we can really use it for at this time.... while I'm sure many developers are working hard to build new and exciting smart contracts right now (and there are a few out already) most people don't even know about them or what they really do so it will take some time before these technologies become mainstream. This isn't necessarily a bad thing because if you know something about computers then you probably realize that features are often added very slowly over time; look at how long it took for any type of web integration to be created on non-operating systems (DOS, Mac OS) for example.

Not only does blockchain technology offer many benefits but it's also much more efficient than the traditional ways we've been doing things... whoever created bitcoin was essentially trying to solve a major problem which is how people can send money to each other online without needing to pay high transaction fees or worrying about things like chargebacks and exchange rates. With that said, I think there are still some issues with this technology at this time - namely scalability. When it comes to things like ethereum, however, the main issue right now is that not enough people actually understand how it works; if you look at reddit then most of these threads are just people talking negatively about the currency rather than providing their reasons as to why they don't like it.

I'm not sure how many people know this but ethereum is actually another type of blockchain. In other words, it's not a new cryptocurrency - ether tokens are used solely for paying transaction fees and smart contracts while the actual currency used by this technology is called gas (which is abbreviated as GAS). The problem I've found with most people talking about ethereum right now, however, is that they're only thinking about buying ether because its price has been going up over the past few months. People should really start thinking about what problems does Ethereum really solve though; so far, we haven't seen anything ground-breaking or revolutionary. That's why I think a lot of projects will continue trying revolution.

OK, so we've covered the basics of bitcoin smart contracts/Dapps now let's take a look at what some people are calling "the next generation" version of these services - EOS (EOS is not actually built on ethereum, it's built on its own blockchain which uses delegated proof-of-stake consensus); this shouldn't come as too much of a surprise because more than 1500 transactions per second can be processed by EOS. You won't find many exchanges that support trading Dapp tokens yet (although there will surely be several available over time) but you will find a few platforms such as Bitfinex and Bitmex which support some forms of Dapp tokens - again, research this for yourself because most of the detailed information is buried in forums which makes it difficult to find unless you know what you're looking for.

I think its very important that you know more about EOS if you really want to be successful as an investor because it's only a matter of time before businesses switch from using ethereum to EOS and they will need platforms that support trading Dapp tokens; at this point, there are no details or official announcements about when/if EOS will start supporting exchanges but by keeping up-to-date with everything taking place surrounding both projects (EOS and ETH), it should be relatively easy to figure out when new developments take place.

11

ARTIFICIAL INTELLIGENCE ON THE BLOCKCHAIN

Artificial Intelligence on the Blockchain

This Chapter explains how AI will likely be used in conjunction with blockchain technology in the future - this article also discusses the issue of trust when it comes to robots (what if they become too smart?) as well as some other issues that need to be addressed before AI can truly be viable on decentralized networks.

Blockchain and Artificial intelligence working together will likely make the future a much better place.

However, a recent report in June 2021 produced by the European Investment Bank and the European Commission, raised concern over the lack of investment of both technologies. It stated that Europe needs to address an investment gap of up to €10 billion that is holding back the development and deployment of artificial intelligence and blockchain technologies in the EU.

The report claims that a lack of investment in the two technologies is restricting economic growth and further innovation. The study found that Europe was trailing behind the US and Asia in these two sectors, with AI software investment far lower than in North America at only €70 million compared to €6 billion."

This chapter attempts to address this issue by highlighting some potential benefits of the synergy between blockchain technology and artificial intelligence. Blockchain technology has had many success stories, but it is still relatively new, while artificial intelligence has been around for decades but never really took off due to lack of widespread adoption. Nowadays, there are converging opinions on the fact that combining both technologies will lead to significant product development opportunities as well as economies-of-scale for businesses looking into these fields.

Some recent advances in blockchain and artificial intelligence have been made:

1. Storiqa - a blockchain-based marketplace for peer-to-peer trading of goods and services with an integrated platform that uses artificial intelligence to tailor business processes. The platform employs smart contracts in the following way: product characteristics, terms and conditions, delivery timescale, after-sales service, etc. are encoded into predefined contracts which can be verified by any third party at any moment during the order fulfilment process; there is no risk for a customer because all agreements are encoded in smart contracts on blockchain so they cannot be modified or tampered with; payment transactions will only be executed upon confirmation from both sides - buyer and seller - once all agreed objectives have been achieved (e.g., once the goods are delivered).

2. Algory Project - an advanced cryptocurrency trading terminal which uses artificial intelligence to increase the efficiency of

crypto traders on a variety of exchanges; it helps with automatic market analysis, price projections as well as asset recommendations based on technical and fundamental indicators. More broadly, the Algory Project aims to change how people look at crypto markets by improving their understanding of these markets; more specifically, it provides detailed information about nearly every altcoin available in circulation, while addressing problems like: high amount of false or misleading information about cryptocurrencies in circulation (i.e., misinformation), lack of transparency during ICOs which leads to loss of investor trust over time - for example, only 10% of all funds raised from ICOs are actually invested in the development of the companies - and lastly, a lack of efficient solutions forcing people to use one exchange for trading while using another for storing coins (i.e., just holding your coins on exchanges leaves you exposed to hacking risks). Such problems can lead to numerous benefits of AI implementation, which will be elaborated upon further on:

a) Automatic market analysis - this means that AI can identify new opportunities or trends in real time based on financial instruments; factors like analyzing historical data (e.g., database with many years worth of information available) as well as current live market events (e.g., transactions happening every second, volumes on different exchanges, possible manipulated market activity etc.) can all be considered in order to find new trends which can then be used by traders who want to try their hand at the crypto markets; AI enabled software is capable of doing all this work on its own, round the clock with virtually no errors, so human traders will not have a chance without using similar bots for themselves.

b) Price projections - very useful feature which allows traders (and other stakeholders interested in the outcome of events such as electronic wallet holders) to see what the future prices are going to look like depending on different factors; AI can analyze historical data and use machine learning algorithms based on it in order to make predictions about cryptocurrency behavior in future situations - e.g., if you hold certain coins then your would like to know if it is better to hold them or sell them to maximize possible profits; if you are considering investing in a new ICO then having an AI tell you what its chances of success look like depending on the amount invested, stage of development etc. would help investors make more informed decisions based on certain criteria which normally they wouldn't have time for - e.g., they can be too busy with work/school and simply don't have enough time to do basic market analysis by themselves...

c) Asset recommendations - very valuable feature as mentioned above because when we speak about trading and investment opportunities, not everyone has the same opportunity costs or restrictions - some people may not want to invest large sums while others may still prefer larger investments in the hopes of generating a higher return; for these people, it is important to find out whether they should invest their existing capital (e.g., hard earned money) into cryptocurrencies or if they should wait until further markets develop so that they can put larger amounts at work; AI implementation would mean that each trader would have access to such kind of data (and possibly more) from a variety of exchanges while taking into account certain criteria which are most relevant in his/her case - i.e., not all people will want to know how price is going to move over the next 2 days because some may be happy with 1 day and others may prefer 90 days.

3. Pecunio - an ICO platform with a direct focus on the gold standard (i.e., investment in real assets); Pecunio will create a crypto/gold investment platform where people can buy shares of companies which are currently mining physical gold; by doing so, investors will receive dividends from their holdings within 1 month of acquiring them (as opposed to traditional offerings

where you need to wait 1-3 years for dividends to kick in) and also benefit from the fact that gold is an inflation hedge (i.e., when your fiat currency loses its purchasing power then all you have done is exchange it for something which has not lost its value - i.e., gold).

4. Investoland - a decentralized peer-to-peer knowledge sharing platform; Investoland will have tutorials, video and text based content for trading on the crypto markets; this means that you can choose to pay particular people for their content or not (i.e., it is free so you are only paying if you really find value in what they are offering); although there are a lot of sites out there which offer such information, many of them do not work as advertised because when money is involved then scammers come out of the woodwork...

5. Hive - an AI/robotics powered one stop shop to offer a wide range of services (e.g., investment advice, legal counseling, technological support) via user's personal digital assistant; imagine being able to speak directly with your advisor about your investment portfolio, being able to ask him/her questions and have your specific answers sent directly to your email address or even better - having it done automatically by robots. This is the future of AI in financial services...it will disrupt the way people interact with financial institutions (i.e., via machines because they are less costly and more efficient).

6. Acorn - an asset management platform with a focus on creating funds where you can invest crypto into real world assets; if you own certain coins then why not use them to purchase real estate, company shares etc.; practical example: you own NEO and believe that its price will go up in value over time - so instead of leaving it on exchanges as fiat which may eventually lose its value, you can exchange it for some of the best performing assets in the world (e.g., real estate) to store your wealth and have a pleasant early retirement at some point

in time; at Acorn, they will help you with this process - from putting your money into an escrow account until it arrives safely at its destination after paying all relevant transaction costs so that all you need to do is sit back and wait...

7. Zeus Exchange - a decentralized peer-to-peer derivatives trading platform; how many times in life did you hear about people complaining about not being able to get rich without taking substantial risks? The truth is that there are more options on the table than just risking everything by investing into a hot IPO on the stock market or buying a lottery ticket with hopes of winning huge amounts (which rarely ever happens); Zeus Exchange is an example of decentralized future where you can benefit from price volatility by entering into smart contracts which will pay out according to certain predefined criteria...

8. EYCHAIN - a payment processing platform for freelancing services; here is how it works - if you are a programmer who writes code and signs it electronically with your personal key in order to release it publicly, after you have done so then all you need to do is make sure that this transaction gets confirmed asap; however, why should Bitcoin miners get paid just because they included your transaction into one block and not another? Therefore, EYCHAIN allows you to pay a small fee in order to guarantee timely confirmation; this means that if you are hired by someone then they can pay their workers automatically via EYCHAIN because it will ensure that your transaction gets confirmed almost instantly...

9. Crypto Currencies Market Data - an open source platform which provides users with real time data about crypto related products; this is the sort of information which people need in order to make better informed decisions (i.e., the Coinranking website, for example, only supplies price and volume stats) whereas for many other things such as - trade history, volume distribution across exchanges, open/close prices etc., one

needs to use a tool like TradingView on its own or on top of another website which provides real-time price updates; we are slowly moving toward a world where all this information will be provided directly from the source (i.e., exchanges themselves) and not via external websites;

10. CryptoCompare - an award winning platform which supplies clients with lots of valuable data - indicators, live charts etc.; in time it could transform into a comprehensive tool for cryptocurrency investors which would provide them with direct access to all of their trading activity by using the API or simply by integrating at least some components directly onto their own website.

Blockchain: the next big thing?

Blockchain technology has already found widespread adoption in several industries such as finance and supply chain management but was mostly known for providing the infrastructure behind Bitcoin, the first decentralized cryptocurrency which came to life around 2009/2010; however, it has been very successful at that task so far. In recent years, there have been rumours that Apple would be incorporating a sort of blockchain technology into their iOS devices - although they denied it - many people believe this will eventually happen given Apple's history with innovation and their position on AI (i.e. Siri).

12

WHAT ARE ICO'S?

What are ICO's?

An in-depth look at what an initial coin offering is and how it works; this chapter also talks about things that you should avoid when it comes investing in them because while some of these projects have great potential, others do not!

I also go into why I think blockchain-based start-ups will eventually replace traditional VC funding as well as crowd funding platforms like Kickstarter and Indiegogo.

What is an ICO/Initial Coin Offering?

In layman's terms, an ICO/initial coin offering is a fundraising instrument where a company releases its own cryptocurrency (tokens) that investors can purchase in exchange for Bitcoin or Ether; interested investors would then be able to trade these coins for other cryptocurrencies like Ethereum and Bitcoin on various exchanges. Although there are some businesses raising capital through ICOs as we speak, this practice isn't new. For example, the first-ever IPO occurred in 1602 where Dutch East India Company sold shares of stock. In the 1990s dot-com bubble era, entrepreneurs around the world created their own internet companies and used IPOs to raise money from individuals across the globe; however, over time, many of these online start-ups failed which resulted in billions of dollars of lost capital.

Introduction To ICOs

Unlike traditional IPOs, initial coin offerings are relatively new; they came into existence around 2013 when Mastercoin (now known as Omni), built on top of the Bitcoin blockchain, tried to do a crowd sale to fund their project and successfully raised more than $500k in 2013 ($760k if you adjust for inflation); this success caught the eye of many entrepreneurs who wanted to create their own tokens/coins but didn't want to go through all the rigorous legal requirements associated with crowd funding at that time. Today there are tens of thousands of different cryptocurrencies available online which investors can purchase using several cryptocurrency exchanges.

ICO's Aren't Always Safe Investments Even though blockchain technology is being used by so many different companies, the majority of ICOs launched are scams; just because a company has a great idea doesn't mean they have an ability to follow through with it. For this reason, you shouldn't blindly invest in any ICO that catches your interest - you should always do your research and make sure what it is exactly that these blockchain-based start-ups are trying to accomplish.

Key Stages of an ICO:

1 - Offer

- This is the first stage of a crowdsale. These firms will pitch their idea to potential investors, list what they plan on doing with all the cryptocurrency raised from their ICO and set a predetermined date where interested parties can purchase tokens/coins using Bitcoin or Ether; in exchange for these cryptocurrencies, investors will receive their new coin/token as well as any bonuses that were offered (usually around 10%).

2 - Pre-sale

- During this period, you'll be able to purchase coins at a lower price than during the initial offers. The same applies here but since there's less money being invested, most of these businesses will offer discounts of up to 20% off the retail price if you invested early (i.e. the more cryptocurrency you buy, the bigger your bonus).

3 - The Public Crowd Sale (ICO)

- Once all coins are sold, these blockchain start-ups will be able to raise capital from a global audience; this is when most companies that are planning an ICO release their whitepaper. This document outlines everything relating to their project including details about how they plan on using any money raised (i.e. development costs, marketing budget and hiring new employees); usually everyone involved with creating the coin/token that's being offered also assists in writing this document so investors know exactly what they're getting themselves into before purchasing their tokens/coins.

4 - Exchange Listing

- After receiving funds, a large portion of developers immediately list their coin/token on cryptocurrency exchanges. However, in order for a token to be listed, they need to meet the requirements set by each exchange (it is at this stage where some companies manipulate their assets and inflate the value of their ICOs).

5 - Aftermarket Trading

- Once your coins are listed on an exchange, you can start buying and selling them at any time; however, most investors tend to hold onto any tokens that have gained in value after listing because there's still a lot of uncertainty regarding whether or not it'll increase in price over time. If your chosen coin ends up being worthless then it won't matter anyways - but if you believe that this project will succeed, then holding onto your shares will result in a quicker exit (i.e. you can sell your coins for more money).

6 - Mainnet Launch and Beyond

- Once a crypto project has raised enough capital to start working on their mainnet, they'll usually launch the official version of their blockchain; these companies will then be able to use their hard-earned funds towards releasing new products/services that run on top of this new network. At this point, your investment in this particular coin/token should start paying off (if it hasn't already). Some people will continue holding onto tokens in hopes that they gain even more value over time while others might dump them once it hits major exchanges - both are valid strategies and investors need to decide what works best for them when deciding whether or not they should HODL.

How to Participate in an ICO

- Do Your Research! Read the Whitepaper, Search for Technical Details on Reddit (i.e. Github) and then Compare it with Other Coins/Tokens that are Listed on Exchanges. Don't just use a simple Google search either; make sure you read all of their white papers, look at each technical document and compare this information with other blockchain start-ups that have performed successful Initial Coin Offerings - if there are any similarities, then your chosen token will probably rise in value over time as well. Don't get too excited over projects that offer very high returns either; chances are that their business models have not been thoroughly tested yet and they haven't had the chance to prove themselves as reliable companies within this industry.

- Look for Cryptocurrency Investors on Twitter, Reddit and YouTube: there are TONS of articles about blockchain technology being published online; if you think this is too much information to sift through then use social media (i.e. search for various crypto influencers). Most people in the cryptocurrency ecosystem like to share interesting links related to their field of expertise - and since most token creators try to spread awareness for their projects by interacting with various members of the community (on Reddit, Slack or Twitter), keep an eye out for anyone who's tweeted about these types of offerings before...it doesn't hurt to start a conversation with them.

- Make Sure You Are Able to Afford the Initial Coin Offering Price: just because you "want" to buy into this ICO doesn't mean that it's smart to invest $10,000+ in tokens if you don't have a lot of money - unless you know for certain that your investment will definitely yield returns, make sure your funds are spread out across multiple projects and never put too much of your savings into any one offering. I've seen many people purchase hundreds or thousands of coins/tokens during crowdsales only to realize months later that they could've purchased more coins/tokens with their initial investment (if they decided against investing in that particular project).

- Understand How Token/Coin Distribution Works: when someone releases a new cryptocurrency token, they'll usually do it by selling their coins to anyone who's interested. Sometimes these offerings will be done through Initial Coin Offerings (ICOs) while other times the tokens are distributed in exchange for goods and services - regardless of which type of crowdsale you participate in, everyone should make sure that they understand how this distribution works so that there aren't any surprises later on.

If you're participating in an ICO then chances are your chosen project is using smart contracts to establish rules about how (and when) you can spend/exchange these coins/tokens; if this is not the case then keep reading because I'll explain more about this topic below.

When you receive coins/tokens through an Initial Coin Offering then your ownership of them is usually defined by a smart contract (i.e. the rules that govern how you can exchange these tokens). For example, if someone releases 10 million tokens and only allows investors to buy 100,000 tokens during their ICO then this means that only 1% of all coins are available for public sale; if they sell out within a few hours then chances are good that early members will profit by selling their stake at a higher price than people who joined later on...and so on).

Regardless of whether or not your chosen token was released during an ICO, it's important to understand what the "total" supply is going to be so that you know for certain whether or not there will be any additional coins/tokens released in the future. If this isn't clear then ask someone from the community who is familiar with these offerings to clarify this information for you - because if a company plans on selling more tokens (e.g. through an Airdrop) then these new coins/tokens could potentially compete with your existing holding when they are introduced into the market...and since most people don't like the idea of competing against their own investments, it's important to do everything possible to avoid being hurt in this way.

- Understand How Regulatory Oversight Works: there are multiple countries that have their own rules regarding blockchain technology and exchanges; however, the majority of countries have not yet established their own rules and regulations for cryptocurrency-related companies, nor is there any indication as of now that they are planning to do so in the near future.

If you live in a country where this oversight has been established then I highly recommend that you always check with your local regulatory agency to see if any specific guidelines or policies exist - while some (or even most) tokens might still be fine under these new laws, there's no doubt that many individuals will want to avoid making investments into certain offerings because they'll either be outlawed entirely or ruled illegal during a later stage in this process.

As an example, here are some of the things I would look up before investing into Token A:

Is Token A legal in my country? (Here's a tool to help answer that question) Is Token A compliant with any existing regulations within my country? Are there ANY indications that the government could ban or outlaw this token at any time in the future? If so, can I/we stop it from happening? Does anyone have an idea where I can find reliable information detailing how these new laws/regulations will be enforced?

If you are not required to check with your local regulatory agency then I still recommend doing all of these things anyway because you never know if Token A may be "banned" on an exchange starting tomorrow...or perhaps someone decides to start listing new tokens and they refuse to list yours regardless of how much community support it has...and so on.

- Understand What Role the Exchange Plays in Your Investment: there is a good chance that you will want to choose an exchange where your tokens can be deposited and exchanged for other coins/tokens, however there are many more factors than just that one!

Does the exchange have any restrictions regarding which countries are allowed to use their platform? Does the exchange list many Ethereum based tokens or do most of them accept Bitcoin instead? Are they located outside of my country so that I don't have to pay taxes when I exchange my currency for Token A? Does this exchange charge high fees (i.e. 0 - 5% per transaction) or even take fees at all? Are the people running this company known in the cryptocurrency community? Do their names appear on LinkedIn and/or can I find old forum posts that mention them? What is the average trading volume of Token A on this exchange in comparison to other exchanges?

I could write a whole separate article about this subject alone, but if you want some in-depth information regarding exchanges then please check out my dedicated post here: Choosing Cryptocurrency Exchanges

- When All Else Fails: if it sounds too good to be true then there's a very large possibility that it isn't an opportunity worth pursuing! This is one of those times where "curiosity killed the cat" because even though you may not know who ran a specific ICO or came up with an idea for a new token/platform, others WILL know and if they're making something that seems a bit fishy then you should probably be extra weary of it.

It's very simple: why do people care about the company behind the ICO? For me personally, I always search for anything related to the team on LinkedIn. If I can't find any information there then I'll look at their YouTube channel (if they have one) or try to find some old forum posts that mention them. If all else fails, I'll simply ask my friends in the crypto community what they've heard about this specific project - I consider online reputation management as one of the most important aspects of token investment because there are so many opportunities out there for scammers, thieves and con artists.

So, what does all of this mean? In a nutshell, if anything sounds too good to be true then it probably is! If you're going to invest into something then you should always do your own due diligence prior to doing so. There's no excuse for naivety or carelessness when it comes to investment because at the end of the day you are willingly putting your money into something that could potentially make you more money than whatever job(s) you have been working on up until this point in time...however there are also a lot of scammy projects out there as well which WILL steal your money and make you regret ever getting involved!

Do I think that the "cryptocurrency community" is as secure as Fort Knox? No...and there are some fantastic articles on Medium that go into more detail regarding this subject, but in this section, I just wanted to emphasize the importance of doing research/due diligence before you invest into any token. If anything looks too good to be true then it probably is , so if it seems like something worth investing in then please take your time and do a lot of digging around first.

- Do Your Own Research: since I've already covered why researching a coin should always be done prior to buying any amount of their tokens or coins (see above), this section will focus specifically on what kinds of information you should be looking at.

There are several other "wisdom of the crowds" systems out there such as wisdomofcrowds .com and icobench , but I personally prefer to do my research by following their social media accounts and reading most/all of their Bitcointalk thread.

While doing your own research is a great way to find projects that could potentially have awesome ROI s, it can also lead you down some very nasty roads when it comes to falling for scams or scams that are more crafty than others. The reason why I feel like this community needs even MORE due diligence is because several scams recently were able to raise millions of dollars in ICO funding (i.e. the recent ATM scam where they raised $375,000 worth of ETH).

It sounds funny for me to say this, but please PLEASE use common sense when it comes to cryptocurrency investing - if you're not feeling like something is safe then don't put your money into it. If I had any sort of inclination that a project was sketchy then I would either wait until later on or just invest smaller amounts. I have never invested more than $100 into an ICO and while this may be pointless for some coins (such as Ethereum), I will keep doing this so that my money doesn't go into complete strangers' hands.

What is a Market cap?

In order for me to explain what a marketcap is, I'm going to compare two of the same coins:

Litecoin ($110.32) - Market Cap is $7,691,173,032 (USD)

Ethereum ($440.54) - Market Cap is $945,422,099 (USD)

What is the difference in their market caps?

The market cap of a coin is calculated by multiplying its price by the total number of coins that will be in circulation when mining ends/the project runs out of tokens to sell. The Ethereum report has a more accurate representation because there's no possibility for an addition of new coins, while Litecoin will continue making new blocks and distributing tokens until about 2040 (I believe that this date could change, though).

How do you determine if something has a good Marketcap or not?

If you're going to invest in cryptocurrency then it's important to understand how everything works, especially since there are so many different factors involved with each individual token. For example, did you know that cryptocurrency market caps vary based on how many people are looking at the market during a given time frame? Well, that's why I was able to find out that Ripple had a 31B USD Marketcap back in February (when it was still worth less than $0.01 per token).

Interesting titbit:

What can you do if you want to invest in cryptocurrency but don't have that much money? The answer is simple...you get 2 or more of your friends to invest with you! From my experience, owning a small amount of cryptocurrency and having it split among multiple people makes the act of trading/investing into something much easier when 1) the price goes down and 2) you need to cash out. For example, let's say that I bought $1000 worth of Dogecoin and my friends each invested $100 with me. If the price per token falls to $0.01, then I only lost 10% while everyone else in our group lost 33%. Now let's assume that you have $500 and are trying to buy 1 BTC. Well if 5 people (that don't know each other) all invest with you, then there's a good chance that you'll be able to purchase it!

If someone were to email or post on a forum asking for money under any circumstance, always do your own due diligence before sending anything their way. Whether they claim they need new parts or coins, be sure to check out Bitcointalk and Google for reviews about them! Even if they were able to post their address on the forums (which is only possible when you have a certain level of trust), scam artists can still get your personal information from this.

Beginning Your Own Coin/Token Sale

If you're looking into starting your own initial coin offering on top of Ethereum's blockchain (it's possible) or you want to start another platform but don't know if there will be enough traffic, the next chapter talks about how to build viral ecosystems using existing technologies like Amazon Web Services and APIs which can attract millions of users over time.

Basics of starting your own ICO:

1. Have a business plan/simulation in order to see if the token's price will go up or down over time. This can be easily done using Excel and by creating charts that reflect the results of your simulations. You should also include certain subjects within your business plan such as scalability, legal issues, security breaches (ex: The DAO hack), etc...

2. Hire developers who are familiar with the blockchain environment or start learning how to code so you can build things on Ethereum yourself! Since no one knows what will happen with cryptocurrency in the future, you might as well learn it now so you have an advantage later on!

3. Build a website and use Amazon Web Services since any other companies charge more money for their services. You can also make your own blockchain token using the Ethereum network, which is explained on their website: ethereum.org/

4. Register a business and get a bank account (or use one from your other businesses).

If you're trying to start up an ICO for Litecoin or Ethereum then it's important that you do thorough research on the different types of blockchains and which ones fit your needs best!

For example, if you don't have enough money to invest in all of the coins that are currently available, you can still make an ICO that will allow users to purchase something with fiat currency.

Once they've purchased their new tokens through credit card or PayPal, they'll be able to send them anywhere without needing a bank account.

For example, someone in the United States could pay for their coffee using Bitcoin if their local café accepts them! This is especially useful since some countries around the world don't have access to banks or they're restricted from making certain transactions with third parties (like buying stocks).

1. Do your research and try to see if there are any new technologies that will come out in the future which could connect with what you want to accomplish.
2. Discuss your plans with as many people as possible and get feedback about them because you'll never know when you might need other resources down the line.
3. Build connections/start relationships early on with government agencies so it'll be easier to find investors later on.
4. Create multiple tiers of users so that the initial investors who purchase different tiers of tokens will discover what all is available for them to purchase.
5. Build an engaging roadmap with a series of numbers which show exactly how many people will be using your platform over time.

13

BLOCKCHAIN CHALLENGES

Blockchain Challenges?

In this chapter, we look at scalability issues that are preventing blockchains from being able to scale to millions or billions of users; then I discuss why scalability is crucial for mass adoption in any technology (along with a short history lesson regarding how TCP/IP was built) finally, I'll provide an updated discussion about things like the Lightning Network, sharding etc. and where these technologies stand today as well as their current limitations.

Here are the main challenges for blockchain technology to overcome:

1. Scalability (tech will need to scale to millions or billions of users)
2. Usability (this stuff isn't exactly user-friendly, even today)
3. Volatility (will need to become less volatile and more stable)

4. Security and Privacy (online security is still a huge problem for most people)
5. Developer Tools (the tools available for app developers are not easy to use or secure)
6. Lack of Use Cases (there is a dire lack of actual applications that currently exist)
7. General Purpose Processing Power (today's tech isn't "general purpose" in any sense of the word, it is optimized for specific tasks like cryptocurrency mining and should likely be viewed as an appliance rather than a general-purpose computing device).

Scalability Challenges - The Proof-of-Work Problem

The problem with scalability on blockchains can generally be boiled down to their reliance on "proof-of-work." In fact, since blockchain technology was first invented, debates have raged over how best to scale it for day-to-day use, with many developers arguing that proof-of-work is the only proven way to achieve decentralization and trustless transactions. Opponents of this view argue that simply because it worked for Bitcoin doesn't mean it will work for other blockchain applications like smart contracts or decentralized file storage systems (e.g. such as Filecoin), and therefore a scalable alternative needs to be found in order for blockchains to reach their full potential.

In this chapter we'll try to understand what exactly "proof of work" is - how it works, why it's important, etc. - then we'll throw around some numbers about how much electricity is used by miners today and talk about alternatives to proof-of-work such as proof-of-stake, delegated proof of stake, and byzantine fault tolerance.

Scalability: Proof of Work vs. Delegated Proof of Stake

In this chapter I'll talk at length about the various mechanisms for achieving consensus in blockchain technology (such as: proof-of-work, Byzantine Fault Tolerance, and so on), then I'll discuss the advantages and disadvantages of each strategy then finally I'll give my personal opinion, which is that DPOS may be the best option for scalability going forward.

Achieving Consensus in Blockchain Technology

The difference between how Bitcoin and Ethereum achieve consensus (or "trustlessness") is quite interesting. While both provide some of the same benefits, such as immutability and resistance to censorship, there are big differences. This section will give you a historical look at what's happened so far with Bitcoin vs. Ethereum.

One of the best things about the blockchain space is how rapidly it's evolving. For example, it wasn't long ago that Ethereum was a proof-of-work chain like Bitcoin -2017 - they've moved to proof-of-stake. How much quicker does this field move than others? Imagine if you released your next smartphone operating system in July 2017 and by December 2017 the group behind Android had already decided on a massive update that would be released in 2018, maybe even with some major changes (not just fixing bugs.) This pace may not be too atypical for cryptocurrency because there are so many people working on these projects full time but what many fail to understand is that there are very few groups who have the resources to do that - for a large company like Apple or Google it's one thing but for an open-source project?

The main difference between Bitcoin vs. Ethereum is this: how they achieve consensus. For Bitcoin, miners use proof-of-work which means they have to solve complex mathematical problems in order to add blocks of new transactions onto the blockchain. In exchange for doing this work, these miners are rewarded with transaction fees and newly minted Bitcoins. Because we know that "electricity = money" then by using PoW, miners are competing on electricity consumption because whoever uses the most power has the best chance of solving the next block thereby earning themselves a nice reward. That, or mining pools are working together to solve these problems, then splitting the rewards among themselves.

The "work" has been referred to as hashing since Bitcoin started using it and because of this, some people think that PoW is a silly use of electricity but at a cost of about $50 billion per year isn't really something you can complain too much about. It's worth mentioning that most servers used for mining aren't specifically designed to be energy efficient so there is definitely some overhead in terms of efficiency here. Now, we all know by now how Ethereum uses proof-of-stake (or POS), right? Not exactly... While they're still using a consensus mechanism called Casper, which uses a partial validating node network, their current implementation is proof-of-work (they're moving to a hybrid) So, how do they achieve this?

Ethereum vs. Bitcoin in Terms of Achieving Consensus

The Ethereum Casper Protocol - What Kind of System Makes a Good Blockchain, Anyway? Understanding the basics behind reaching consensus for blockchains is something that takes time but it's also an important concept to grasp if you want state-of-the-art knowledge on the subject. The most common types of consensus mechanisms are as follows: Proof of Work (PoW) This means miners are competing against each other for rewards by using more powerful computers and consuming massive amounts of electricity. The main benefit of this strategy to prevent Sybil attacks by making it expensive to forge identities. This system has been used since the beginning of Bitcoin and is still in use today even though there are much better alternatives available. Proof of Stake (PoS) The idea here is a lot more simple although the actual process for achieving consensus will vary from cryptocurrency to cryptocurrency. Here, users who own coins in a network are able to mine with their wallets instead of investing money into super powerful miners. Those who held the most coins also have the highest chance of mining new blocks first. Delegated Proof of Stake (DPoS) This type of system involves token holders voting on delegates who can build blocks on top of a blockchain. These are usually called witnesses or forgers, which means that they are responsible for signing blocks and adding them to the blockchain. They're called witnesses because of their ability to verify transactions, store data in an append only public ledger as well as mine new blocks.

Byzantine Fault Tolerance

(BFT) This is a protocol that ensures consensus on a distributed system. It's based on the idea of reaching an agreement between nodes or peer-to-peer participants despite being under stress and faults. Practically, it's about running a node or wallet and having each participant agree with what transpires in the network. Multi-PPS (MCPoW) In this model, multiple miners will be rewarded for finding new blocks in a form of lottery. The only thing that matters here is the total hashrate of all miners combined rather than how much work (or electricity) they're using to reach those goals.

This area still has some more testing to do since there are limits to PoS but Ethereum seems excited about it so it should be interesting to see where this goes.

Brace yourselves... We're about to talk about Sharding! While there are a lot of people who like the idea of sharding, many experts believe they'll find difficulty building on top of Ethereum until they have Casper in place. If you want to know more about what sharding is and why everyone is talking about it, make sure you check out their official FAQ . It can get pretty complex but if you put some effort into researching solid explanations for both PoS and PoW, you should come up with some good resources, which explain how these things work in much deeper detail than I could ever provide.

Essentials of Byzantine Fault Tolerance:

Essentially, this is about how to send signals and messages between two parties who have to come together in order to coordinate an attack, for example. In a protocol like Bitcoin, nodes that are not operating within the system's rules will be identified as malicious which means they don't receive any form of reward in return for sharing their blocks (transactions). While there are a lot of ways to prevent this from happening, it's still very hard to guarantee consensus on whether or not someone is acting "within spec" because you'd need everyone involved in a transaction to agree with what's going on.

In most cases, the only way you can solve this is by running node software and hashing until all parties come to an agreement. However, you still need a way to verify that all nodes are following the same rules, which is where Byzantine Fault Tolerance comes into play.

The group will try to come up with an answer and while they must reach consensus before they can move forward (and be rewarded), there's no guarantee they'll actually succeed without picking one person or group of people who just goes ahead and does things. This is where "Byzantine" comes into play since it refers to hypothetical characters who could behave maliciously in order for them to solve the problem on their own terms regardless of what anyone else thinks. There are strategies in place, which assume this is always possible but a lot of people believe its only effective against small nodes. It's a very complicated subject and chances are high that you won't have the answer until you get involved in Bitcoin or another altcoin (with protocol rules).

Cycles (referred to as "epochs" in Ethereum's case) are used for generating PoW. These will only happen after a certain amount of time has passed unless there's an event like a hack or someone trying to take control over more than half of the network's hashing power. In any event, this is basically how Ethereum plans on solving their scalability issue by allowing transactions to be processed at different speeds based on what type of transaction it is.

Advantages and Disadvantages of each Strategy:

PoW (proof-of-work)

Disadvantages: you need to invest in hardware and/or time and energy, it's expensive which is why miners have been able to earn so much money from mining pools. It also takes a lot of time for each block, the longest being around 16 hours for Bitcoin and about 12 seconds for Litecoin.

Examples:

1. Bitcoin: 10 minutes - 2 weeks+ (2 blocks per hour)

2. Litecoin: 2. 5 minutes - 4 days + (5 blocks per hour) [citation needed] 3. Ethereum: 15-20 seconds - ~26 days (+0. 0451% chance per block)

2. Litecoin: 2.5 minutes - 10 minutes (25 blocks per hour)

3. Dash: 1 minute - 10 minutes (600 blocks per hour)

4. Dogecoin: ~1 minute - 10 minutes (600 blocks per hour)

Advantages: it prevents spam, it prevents the scenario in which one person could control more than 50% of the network and reverse transactions, it's just about impossible to hack proof, you can verify that all miners are adhering to protocol rules by compiling transactions into a block and hashing them until they give an answer which is acceptable to everyone taking part in the transaction validation process. In fact, this is what keeps Bitcoin from being hacked since smart contracts need time-stamped transactions to be "activated" in order for the blockchain (smart contract) to complete its intended function.

Disadvantages: it's very costly, requires a lot of energy since ASICs must be used for miners to compete and get a reward, consensus is always challenging considering that you need more than 50% or 40% hashing power if you want to attempt a hack which is why decentralization plays such an important part in the validation process, all nodes must agree on what happened within each 10-minute block which is no easy feat. Oftentimes node software will simply malfunction and not report certain things until they're discovered by others shortly afterward.

PoS (proof-of-stake)

Disadvantages: it's less secure, 51% attacks are still possible though they're much more costly and difficult to accomplish, you can only mine with a certain amount of coins so if the price goes up or down, it affects your mining ability.

Examples:

1. Peercoin: 1% interest per year - 2.5 minutes (25 blocks per hour)
2. Nxt : 1% interest per year - 1 minute (60 blocks per hour)

3. Ripple: 0. 0005XRP as a base reward with transaction fees included,

100B coins total staking possible at the moment but only 10% have been activated, 100-second confirmation times

Advantages: it's much cheaper since no hardware must be purchased, all nodes (users/investors of a particular cryptocurrency blockchain) are required to take part in order for validation to occur which means sharing computer resources and electricity bills, it requires far less time and energy since time is cut by more than half at the very least without increasing network

DPOS Best Option for Scalability

DPOS (delegated proof-of-stake) this is by far the best option for scalability since no mining is involved, it's extremely fast and fair, only those who take part (have coins to stake) can validate transactions because they're required to prove that they own said coins in order to be granted permission.

Disadvantages: you need a lot of capital if you plan on joining the network as a validator because this will determine how much voting power, you'll have which determines your chances of being selected and also rewarding you with transaction fees every time someone sends cryptocurrency via your node during block validation.

Advantages: speed is increased drastically compared to PoW or PoS so confirmation times are less than 10 -15 seconds depending on the platform, nodes must be online 24/7 otherwise, they'll be kicked from the network and won't receive any transaction fees for that particular day. This makes for a far more honest approach since validators will always be working hard to keep their nodes up and running at all times, if they're not in sync with the rest of the network then it's a wasted effort on their behalf which means that uptime is crucial.

Disadvantages: there are no such things as "instant transactions" because you have to wait for block confirmation before your coins are sent/receive d, this isn't feasible for payments unless you're willing to wait minutes or even hours depending on the cryptocurrency (crypto currency) used , slow block times also mean slow transfer rates which could result in a huge backlog of transactions since you'd have to wait for multiple blocks to be validated before one has the chance to move forward, this means that any sort of application which requires immediate feedback is not going work.

Addressing Scalability Issues with Blockchain

If scalability can't be addressed by enlarging the block size limit, then it may have to come from another avenue. The most promising option would seem to be sharding. Sharding divides all transactions into equal groups called "shards" and puts them onto different shards according to whatever rules are defined within the blockchain's code. This way there is no need for massive amounts of information because each transaction will only provide relevant info (i.e.: source & destination address/s). Each shard would be processed by a different node since it's independent.

Potential Issues: no one shard will hold all the information so there must be some sort of way to communicate between them, this creates a security risk because nodes could theoretically manipulate data and other such things. There also needs to be a verification process or checkpoint, which confirms that transactions are being handled properly. One possible solution is what Ethereum plans on implementing in their new Casper update, using "checkpoints" (pre-selected addresses) somewhere within the blockchain code where every cryptocurrency transaction must pass through for validation. If any hacker tries to change anything then they'll simply invalidate said block(s). But even with this system in place there is still the issue of public vs. private blockchain networks and how they interact with one another.

Getting to Know Ethereum's Casper

Casper FFG is the first step in ethereum's transition from PoW (proof-of-work) to PoS(proof-of-stake). In order to prevent a fork, Casper uses "validators" whose job it is to propose, validate and finalize blocks. Anyone can be a validator simply by depositing ETH into the smart contract, this ensures that no bad actors will have access because they'll need an enormous amount of ETH before being able to stake theirs for a chance at validation however, even though anyone can do this there is still a ranking system which determines who actually gets the chance since not everyone has an equal number of coins. This is to prevent any sort of "rich get richer" effects from happening, it also prevents network spam and keeps the risk/cost of staking relatively low because anyone who tries to attack the blockchain will have most likely already lost their stake in doing so.

Final Thoughts: Casper's sharding solution looks like a good way for bitcoin & other cryptocurrencies alike to scale with little loss (if any) in transaction speed or confirmation times but even still there are some issues which haven't been addressed yet, such as how do you tell whether one block hasn't been tampered with when compared to another? It seems that it may be more hassle than its worth and you're better off just sticking with PoW.

As of right now blockchain technology is still in its infancy, it's only been around since 2008 and there's a lot more work to be done before we have a fully functional, widely adopted cryptocurrency (crypto currency) but I'm sure someday soon the world will start to see what all the hype is about.

14

Blockchain Applications In Other Industries

Blockchain Applications in Other Industries

In this chapter we look at where blockchains may be adopted next including: supply chain management, medical records and other applications that can be improved by switching to a decentralized model for information storage & distribution. Supply Chain Management for example, has been identified as an area ripe for disruption by blockchain technology due to its potential ability to help suppliers; manufacturers and all of their customers better coordinate their actions. Today when a consumer goes to the grocery story, they have no way of knowing if the tuna fish they're purchasing is actually sustainable or even if it's really tuna fish at all. If we could use blockchain tech to create an open & transparent supply chain for food products this would benefit everyone - farmers, grocers, distributors & most of all consumers (who would know that what they were buying was both organic and authentic). In other industries as well, there are tons of opportunities to reduce costs, increase efficiency and eliminate needless bureaucracy by switching over to a decentralized model such as shared databases used across many different companies or parties.

This means that the information on these databases is public, easily accessed and editable by all parties. In other words: no more central database! The blockchain offers a range of advantages over traditional centralized databases including security, transparency and most importantly, cost-effectiveness (since there's no need for third party intermediaries like banks & lawyers to facilitate transfers between actors in the network).

This raises a major question: if blockchains can be used to store sensitive information like medical records why do we even need to rely on centralized organizations such as doctors & hospitals? This leads us to ask even further questions about how exactly data will flow between different parties when deployed into actual use cases. Today your doctor usually knows more about you than anyone else does - who owns that information? How will it be stored and who gets to see it? If you are in a life-or-death situation what happens if you can't get access to your data - how do we prevent this from happening?

A shared blockchain database which is easily accessible by all parties in the network solves this problem because it's easy to see who's trying to access your data and why. In theory, at least, smart contracts could be used to allow doctors or other medical staff to view vital information about your health, however they cannot make any changes unless authorized by you or another party that has permission.

Because blockchains are encrypted & decentralized it is often difficult for hackers & fraudsters to gain access to them - a protection which makes blockchain technology particularly attractive to industries such as: healthcare where patient privacy is paramount. Additionally, if records were stored on a blockchain (instead of left vulnerable on centralized servers) then even if hackers did manage to gain access, they wouldn't be able to do much with them since they aren't able to modify the information stored.

Blockchain technology can also be used in many types of voting systems such as for selecting board members, making executive decisions or choosing which charities receive funding from a foundation (for example). This makes it highly resistant to hacking attempts and ensures that votes cannot be tampered with once cast during an election. Vote rigging & manipulation has been a major challenge in countries all over the world including Kenya, Sierra Leone and recently America were large sums of money have reportedly been spent attempting to corrupt voting results through local power brokers (as illustrated by Russian interference in recent U.S elections). By using blockchain tech we ensure democracy is upheld and nobody is able to alter vote counts without being caught.

Key Blockchain Use in Other Applications:

- Healthcare: as we mentioned in the previous section, blockchain technology can be used to store medical records & other sensitive information in a secure and easily accessible location. This could save billions of dollars in healthcare costs as it becomes easier to share data between doctors & patients and eliminate the need for expensive third-party intermediaries.
- Supply Chain Tracking: Knowing where your food or consumer goods come from has never been more important with all the scandals surrounding poor animal welfare practices at a number of large-scale farms.
- International Payments: transferring money abroad is often extremely time consuming (especially if you have to wait for multiple parties such as banks to verify funds) however this problem could be solved by using cryptocurrency systems which rely on blockchain

technology. The system is also is cheaper so this could benefit consumers everywhere.

- Voting: blockchain technology has already been used to cast votes for the upcoming elections in Sierra Leone. This new system provides an affordable & secure voting service which ensures that no one can tamper with ballots after they have been cast (it's extremely cheap as well). The technology has even been implemented by Estonia - a country ranked #1 globally when it comes to government e-services.

- Insurance: Blockchains make it easier to track claims & detect fraud because records are easily accessible and stored on a network visible to multiple parties. By using smart contracts, we can easily control who gets access to sensitive information such as medical data or financials of customers who are making insurance claims.

- Identity: a blockchain system can be used to verify the identities of people, potentially eliminating fraud and identity theft from an industry that loses billions per year.

- - Forex Trading: there are multiple companies who are looking into providing decentralized trading as a service through blockchains such as Bancor or Waves which will remove the need for third party brokers when trading currencies. This would make it cheaper & safer to trade funds internationally while also ensuring your money remains safe (because you hold the private keys).

There are numerous other use cases for blockchain technology including in supply chain management, insurance, fundraising & many other industries. It is worth mentioning however that certain applications may not require "full" blockchains - instead they could benefit from a hybrid model where blockchains are used to verify and validate transactions which can then be written into a regular database. This is known as an "Enterprise Blockchain" and has been implemented by a number of large companies.

Blockchain technology has already found its way into multiple industries and promises to improve the lives of billions of people in the coming years by making systems more efficient, cheaper & secure. If you want to learn more, we recommend taking a look at some existing blockchain businesses or researching current trends/projects within this area.

- Blockchain as a Service: BaaS or 'Blockchain as a Service' refers to cloud-based applications where you can rapidly deploy blockchains without having servers of your own. Initially these blockchain systems usually only include basic features however they are relatively cheap to use and could be sufficient for certain applications. This is especially true for ERC20 tokens which allow you to create digital value within the Ethereum network (built on top of the bitcoin blockchain) - it costs around 1/2 $0.10 per transaction so you'll probably want to use this in situations where security needs to be kept at a minimum even though it's also possible to use this system for more complex applications. The most popular choice is currently ether. camp, it's free and easy to use so we recommend trying that out if you're serious about getting into blockchain development!
- NEM: an example of a common platform where you can deploy your own blockchain application is NEM (based on the peercoin protocol). This platform allows you to build custom blockchains in just minutes by following some simple tutorials - although it has lower security than Ethereum (i.e., less nodes verify information) so it's not suitable for all projects. However, deploying an application on this blockchain costs around $0 .01 per

transaction which could make it useful in certain situations, maybe as a part of another larger blockchain system (such as the hybrid enterprise model mentioned earlier).

- Ethereum: one of the most popular choices for blockchain development is probably Ethereum (which uses a modified version of the peercoin protocol). It's currently by far the easiest platform to deploy blockchains on - you can create your own in just minutes, without having any servers & with relatively little programming experience. However, be ready to spend some money because running applications on this system costs around $0.03 per transaction which could quickly add up if you're working with large amounts of data or processing numerous transactions at once. This is still much cheaper than traditional server hosting options so it will likely remain a very common choice until new/cheaper alternatives arise. You can get an idea about what developers have been building on this platform by visiting the top projects page on github (it's currently home to thousands of blockchain applications). - Other Options: there are many other options that you could investigate further including Hyperledger, Multichain & Ethereum Classic. If you just want to get started with a simple project, we recommend trying out NEM first then progressing onto Ethereum if necessary.

A good place to start learning about blockchains would be www.blockchainhub.net - they have lots of useful guides and tutorials about how this technology works as well as information about existing platforms and some interesting use cases for future development. They also have an active community which is a great place to ask questions!

Other popular/useful links for anyone interested in exploring this topic further could include:

- ropsten.ether.camp/ - the dashboard for Ethereum's Ropsten test blockchain (it also includes a block explorer). Here you can visualise and analyse transactions which is useful for testing your own apps before launching them on the main network. Note that it will probably take some time to sync before you can use it properly, we recommend using an external client.

CONCLUSION

Final Thoughts on the Future of Blockchain Technology

The truth is that the full potential of this technology has likely only just begun to be explored. We are still in the early days of blockchain development and it's hard to predict how this technology will develop in years to come but there is no doubt that it has a very bright future ahead of itself. Some people have described it as "space travel for money", predicting that it could someday become more efficient than traditional payment systems (and even take over from more traditional databases in some situations).

Looking back at the history of other recent technological revolutions, sometimes small projects with a simple idea can quickly snowball into something much bigger - we've seen this happen with projects like Kickstarter which originally started out as a way to fund individual creative projects/businesses but is now being used by big companies to fund their new products.

A few popular Kickstarter projects were later picked up and turned into huge global enterprises with hundreds of employees and millions of customers. This has happened many times in the past including things like Slack, AirBnB, Reddit & Hotmail/Outlook - all of them started out as small side projects that quickly became something much bigger (a lot of people would say they changed the world). Blockchain technology could have a similar impact if it catches on!

In order for this "revolution" to happen we will need to see some major changes though - proof-of-work mining is likely unsustainable if blockchain development continues at such a rapid pace so hopefully we'll start to see better alternatives (such as proof-of-stake) emerge soon. It's also not very scalable and developers have been working hard to figure out new ways to make it more efficient.

At the same time even big companies like IBM are getting involved with this technology - they recently launched a blockchain solution for global trade which could be a major step toward mainstream adoption of blockchain technology. If these changes happen then blockchains could become an important part of our online infrastructure in future years moving us away from things like centralised servers, middlemen servers/services and distributed denial of service attacks (DOS attacks).

There is also a lot of potential for using blockchains to create new kinds of peer-to-peer marketplaces which would allow buyers and sellers to exchange things without needing any middlemen (see the next section for more information about this).

It's still very early days so it is important to be realistic here but these are some of the exciting directions that blockchain technology could take in the future!

The potential of the technology behind blockchain is certainly very exciting and it is one of the reasons why blockchain development has become so popular over the last few years. However, there are still some significant challenges faced by developers working on this technology which we've discussed previously in greater detail throughout this book.

There are many different types of blockchain architecture being developed at the moment with various pros/cons for each approach. As a general rule however, most blockchains today can be broken down into one of two groups: permissionless or permission. Permissionless blockchains allow anyone to read, send transactions and participate in consensus whereas with permissioned blockchains only certain nodes within a private network have these permissions.

Various companies have been testing different kinds of blockchain architectures including Ripple, Hyperledger & Ethereum. It possible that the future might involve some kind of hybrid approach where permissioned blockchains are used to build private chains/networks while public permissionless blockchains are used to create connections between them (similar to how things work today with the internet).

One of the key advantages of using blockchain technology is that it can be used to process payments much more quickly and cheaply compared with traditional payment systems. This is because in most cases there aren't any middlemen taking a cut during each transaction so transactions costs could potentially become very low in future.

Another advantage is that blockchain ledgers offer increased transparency and it could become easier for governments and other organisations to spot fraudulent behaviour and prevent money laundering. In theory, blockchain technology could even be used to prevent governments from tracking/monitoring payments which might make it harder to regulate cryptocurrencies in the future.

Of course, blockchain technology is still in its early days so we need to see how things develop moving forward but this is a pretty realistic description of what the future might look like if blockchains end up having a similar impact as other technologies such as the internet (which was also originally met with some scepticism by many people).

The potential for using blockchains for creating new kinds of marketplaces is certainly very interesting since it could open up more opportunities for people trying to sell their products online.

People across the globe are increasingly turning towards peer-to-peer exchanges thanks to sites like eBay & Amazon.

In sum, the future of blockchain technology is still very uncertain but there are some exciting possibilities ahead of us. Hopefully we'll see much bigger changes in the near future and blockchains will become an important part of our online infrastructure!

www.ingramcontent.com/pod-product-compliance
Ingram Content Group UK Ltd.
Pitfield, Milton Keynes, MK11 3LW, UK
UKHW041640190726
13854UKWH00006B/2617

9 781915 002020